Seriously Good
Soups

Seriously Good
Soups

Over 60 Recipes,
for Seriously Good Soup

Rebecca Woods

Photography by Luke Albert

Quadrille

Quadrille, Penguin Random House UK, One Embassy Gardens, 8 Viaduct Gardens, London SW11 7BW

Quadrille Publishing Limited is part of the Penguin Random House group of companies whose addresses can be found at global.penguinrandomhouse.com

Penguin
Random House
UK

Published by Quadrille in 2025

First published as *Nourish Soups* in 2017 by Quadrille, an imprint of Hardie Grant Publishing

www.penguin.co.uk

A CIP catalogue record for this book is available from the British Library

ISBN 9781837833153
10 9 8 7 6 5 4 3 2 1

Managing Director: Sarah Lavelle
Senior Commissioning Editor: Stacey Cleworth
Project Editors: Céline Hughes and Sofie Shearman
Copy Editor: Corinne Masciocchi
Series Designer: Katy Everett
Designer: Alicia House
Photographer: Luke Albert
Food Stylist: Rebecca Woods
Prop Stylist: Agathe Gits
Head of Production: Stephen Lang
Production Controller: Sumayyah Waheed

Colour reproduction by F1

Printed in China by C&C Offset Printing Co., Ltd.

The authorised representative in the EEA is Penguin Random House Ireland, Morrison Chambers, 32 Nassau Street, Dublin D02 YH68.

Penguin Random House is committed to a sustainable future for our business, our readers and our planet. This book is made from Forest Stewardship Council® certified paper.

MIX
Paper | Supporting responsible forestry
FSC® C018179
FSC
www.fsc.org

Contents

Introduction

'Who doesn't love soup?' was the response most often received from friends and family when I told them the subject of this book. It turns out that everyone is surprisingly effusive on the matter of soup. The rows and rows of cartons and cans of ready-made soup in supermarket aisles and chillers are testament to its belovedness. In fact, I suspect we're suspicious of anyone who claims not to eat soup at least once in a while.

Perhaps this is because it's tricky to dislike something that can literally be anything you want it to be. And to get all etymological on you, that's the whole point – 'soup', in its original sense, is a jumble, a mixture of different elements. You can add anything you like, to make it fit for any occasion – a light brothy starter in an Asian style on a summery day, or a hearty warming wintery mix, packed with satisfying grains and tender meat. But whatever you choose, it's never better than when you make it yourself… and there are few foods that won't taste good when suspended in a bowl of delicious broth.

But it goes beyond flavour, too; for me, soup is a food that is so inextricably intertwined with growing up – from a bowl of chicken soup on a sick day or a can of cream of tomato (there's a reason Warhol immortalized this) with a cheese toastie as a child, to a pot of noodly pho enjoyed on a plastic stool at the side of a Hanoi street, those happy memories bring comfort. It has unequalled nostalgic power that will ground you, not just physically, but emotionally, too.

I've tried to rein in my classic French cookery training and bring a healthy slant to the recipes here. They are wholesome, packed with fresh vegetables, whole grains and, for the most part, lean proteins. While a few liberties have been taken with a smidgen of butter, a drizzle of cream or a splash of alcohol here and there for that all-important flavour, on the whole I have kept them as concoctions that will leave you feeling nourished and energized, satisfied not soporific.

'Are there even 60 soup recipes?' one friend asked. Well, that's rather the point. There are as many as you want there to be. Let this book be just a starting point.

A Few
Hints & Tips

One of the joys of soup is its simplicity. There's very little that you need in the way of equipment or even cooking expertise. But there are a few hints and tips that might help you along the way, especially if you decide to go off-piste and devise your own soup concoctions rather than strictly following the recipes here – something I wholeheartedly encourage.

Quality Ingredients

The simplicity of many of the soups here means that often they are only as good as their ingredients, especially when it comes to meat and fish. Try to buy the best produce that you can afford and your soup will be all the better for it. You can, of course, be a little more flexible with veggies – puréed soups are one of the best ways to be economical and use up vegetables that are a little past their best.

Brothy or Creamy?

While a thick puréed and spiced root veg soup might be an ideal warmer-upper for a cold day, a light vegetable or seafood broth makes a great summer starter. There's no need to pick a favourite, but it's worth investing in a proper blender/ liquidizer if you are going to be making lots of puréed soups – for speed and smoothness. Stick immersion blenders are great for partially blending soups to thicken them (see overleaf), but there will probably always be lumps that make it through if you're trying to blend the whole pan. Of course, many of the soups here have been left as broths, especially those including meat, which is less suitable for blending, and are better as hearty, stewy soups.

Cooking Times

I've tried to include a mixture of methods, some very quick and simple, and others that depend on a more lengthy cooking process. While some of the cooking processes may seem a bit drawn out, sometimes there's no shortcut to deep flavour and tender meat (or beans in the case of the Slow-baked Greek Bean Soup with Halloumi Croutons on page 101). Once a slow-cooked soup is bubbling away, it doesn't really need a lot of attention, so don't see it as extra work. It will also fill the house with deliciously comforting smells.

Adding Flavour

Keeping a basic store cupboard of liquid seasonings – such as soy sauce, Worcestershire sauce, balsamic vinegar, Tabasco, etc. – and dried herbs and spices means you will have plenty of tools to add a hit of flavour, should your soup need perking up a little. If you can find space in the garden or on the windowsill for a few pots of fresh herbs, too, their power can't be overstated.

A Word on Seasoning

For most healthy adults, seasoning food properly is not a health hazard. At the risk of antagonizing cardiologists everywhere, I'm inclined to believe that if you're enjoying freshly cooked homemade food at each meal of the day and keeping processed meals and snacks to an absolute minimum, it's very unlikely that you will be consuming too much salt by adding it to your soups, and the flavour will suffer if you don't use it. Season sagely…

Thickening

If you're making a soup in which the main ingredient is a vegetable, especially a green, leafy one with a high water content, you'll need something to thicken it so that it feels more substantial. Potato is classically used for this, but I'm also a big fan of using rice, which adds a different, delicate flavour to the soup. You can also use cornflour (cornstarch), slaked with a drop of water then added back into the soup and cooked for a few minutes, like I have in the Coconut & Lemongrass Malay Squash Chowder on page 150. Or, you can simply blend a little of the soup (with a stick blender or by blitzing a little in a blender and returning it to the pan) and the small proportion of puréed solids will add body.

Stock

I'm not a huge fan of dehydrated stock cubes. Sometimes, there's just no hiding that artificial tang they seem to imbue everything with, especially in more delicately flavoured soups, such as asparagus. Although, if you are adding lots of spices or starchy vegetables to a soup, they are usually fine, and are admittedly a lot cheaper than other options. I have provided the following recipes for basic stocks for meat, fish and vegetables, but if time is short, I know corners do need to be cut. Do try to use either a pot or pouch of ready-made stock, or at least the jelly stock pots, which don't seem to be so processed in flavour as the dried cubes. Several of the recipes have a stock written into the recipe, which it is best to follow for the optimum flavour – and to properly (slow) cook any meat or fish in the soup.

Meat

Stock

 Makes about 1.5 litres (6 cups)

 TAKES 3 hrs

1.5kg (3¼lb) chicken or beef bones or
    carcasses (depending on the recipe)
a little olive oil, to drizzle
2 large carrots, peeled and chopped
    into chunks
1 large onion, halved
2 celery sticks, chopped into chunks
1 large leek, chopped into chunks
a bouquet garni made up of parsley
    stalks, thyme sprigs and a bay leaf
a few black peppercorns

Preheat the oven to 190°C fan/375°F/Gas 5.

Put the bones into a large roasting pan and drizzle with a little oil – not too much or you will have a fatty stock. Toss the bones to coat them in the oil, then roast for about 30 minutes until the bones are browned. You can skip this step and put the bones straight in the saucepan with the water, if you wish, but roasting the bones really does help bring out their meaty flavour.

Put the bones in a large saucepan, leaving any fat in the roasting pan, and add all the remaining ingredients. Cover with about 2.5 litres (10 cups) of cold water, set the pan over a medium heat, cover loosely with a lid and bring the stock up to a simmer.

Once the stock is almost boiling, skim any scum from the surface with a large spoon. (Keep the spoon and a bowl at the side of the pan so you can skim it occasionally during cooking.) Reduce the heat to low and cook for about 2 hours, loosely covered, until well flavoured.

Strain the stock through a fine strainer to remove the bones and aromatics. Now you can transfer it to a clean saucepan and continue to cook it down to intensify the flavour, or simply put it in the fridge or freezer until needed.

Fish
Stock

 Makes about 1 litre (4 cups)

 TAKES at least 30 mins

1 tbsp butter
1 onion, diced
1 fennel bulb, sliced
150ml (⅔ cup) white wine
1.25kg (2¾lb) white fish heads and bones or prawn (shrimp) shells, washed of any blood (don't use oily fish for stock)
a bouquet garni made up of parsley stalks, thyme sprigs and a bay leaf

Melt the butter in a large saucepan and gently sauté the onion and fennel for 5 minutes or so until well softened and translucent. Add the white wine and fish bones and cover with about 1.5–2 litres (6–8 cups) cold water – enough to just cover the bones.

Set the pan over a medium heat, cover loosely with a lid and bring the water slowly up to a simmer. Once it is just about at boiling point, reduce the heat to low and leave to simmer gently for 20 minutes.

Strain the stock through a fine strainer to remove the fish bones and aromatics. Now you can transfer it to a clean saucepan and continue to cook it down to intensify the flavour, or simply put it in the fridge or freezer until needed.

Vegetable
Stock

 Makes about 1.5 litres (6 cups)

 TAKES 30 mins

2 large onions, peeled and roughly diced
3 large carrots, thickly sliced
2 large leeks, thickly sliced
2 celery sticks, thickly sliced
2 whole garlic cloves, peeled
1 large fennel bulb, roughly chopped
a bouquet garni made up of parsley stalks, thyme sprigs and a bay leaf
a few black peppercorns

Put everything into a large saucepan and cover with about 1.5 litres (6 cups) of water. Set the pan over a medium heat, cover loosely with a lid and bring the water slowly up to the boil. Once it is just about at boiling point, reduce the heat to low and leave to simmer gently for 30 minutes.

Strain the stock through a fine strainer to remove the vegetables and aromatics, then store in a container in the fridge or freezer until required.

Soup
Toppers

Nuts & Seeds

Nuts and seeds, especially toasted ones, are a great healthy way to add a bit of extra flavour and texture to soups and boost their nutritional value, too. Hazelnuts, almonds, cashews, walnuts, pine nuts and pumpkin, hemp and watermelon seeds have all been suggested throughout the book, but don't feel limited to these. Experiment and sub in whatever you think may work – or whatever opened packets you have lurking at the back of the cupboard…

Drizzles

Herb-based sauces such as pesto, chimichurri and salsa verde make a great last-minute addition, drizzled over the final soup. Adding herbs like this, post cooking, keeps their fresh punchy flavour, which can lift a soup.

Likewise, using strongly flavoured oils such as toasted sesame, walnut or hazelnut oils; extra virgin olive oil; or oils that have been flavoured with chilli or lemon, for example, can add depth and richness to the soup. And never underestimate the power of a good squeeze of lime or lemon juice to lift flavour.

Shoppable Toppers

A stroll around the supermarket aisles reveals plenty of other choices for things that can add interest to a humble soup.

Shop the chilled aisle for crème fraîche, soured cream or Greek yogurt to cool down spicy soups, or cheeses such as Stilton, Parmesan or goat's cheese to add a sharpness to richer ones.

Shards of crisp golden bacon, tiny scallops or ribbons of smoked salmon help an everyday bowl of soup feel a bit more of an occasion and add a protein boost that can turn it from a light lunch into a satisfying meal.

Crispy fried onions or salted popcorn add a pleasing crunch, or you could even try a handful of granola over smooth wintery soups, such as pumpkin or mushroom. Shop with an open mind!

Finally, fresh ingredients such as herbs, rocket (arugula), sliced radishes (pickled or not – see page 28), or just some lemon or lime zest finely grated over the top can all help you to easily customize your soup to reflect how you feel that day.

Finishing off a bowl of soup with a sprinkle of something not only makes it more appealing to the eye and adds extra flavour, but also adds textural contrast – useful if you've made a more homogeneous blended soup. There are endless possibilities to add that bit of complementary flavour and texture.

Classic
Croutons

 SERVES 4–6

 TAKES 15 mins

3 thick slices of sourdough bread, cut
 into cubes
2–3 tbsp olive oil
sea salt flakes

Preheat the oven to 190°C fan/375°F/Gas 5. Put the bread in a large bowl and drizzle over the olive oil. Season well with the sea salt flakes and toss everything together so that the bread is well coated in the oil. Spread the cubes out on a baking sheet and bake for 10–12 minutes, stirring halfway through, or until turning golden and crispy.

Cheesy
Polenta Croutons

 SERVES 4–6

 TAKES 20 mins

100g (⅔ cup) fine polenta (cornmeal)
1 tsp sea salt flakes (use less if using fine salt)
50g (¾ cup) finely grated Parmesan
25g (2 tbsp) butter

Put the polenta in a saucepan with 400ml (1¾ cups) of water and heat over a low–medium heat, stirring all the time, until it comes to the boil. Once boiling, cook, still stirring constantly, for about 6–7 minutes until smooth and no longer grainy. Stir in the salt, Parmesan and butter and cook for another couple of minutes until the butter and cheese have melted. Tip the polenta on to a non-stick baking sheet and form into a square roughly measuring 18 x 18cm (7 x 7in) and about 1.5cm (⅝in) thick. Leave to cool and set.

To finish the croutons, turn out the block of polenta and cut it into 1.5cm (⅝in) dice. Heat a non-stick (this is essential – don't try this in anything without a non-stick coating) frying pan over a medium–high heat and fry the polenta cubes, a few at a time, until they are golden brown on all sides.

Light &
Refreshing

Charred Corn, Peppers and Pineapple
Jerk Chicken Soup

The surprise star here turns out to be the lowly, unsuspecting slice of pineapple lurking at the back of the fridge. I originally thought that an injection of acidic fruitiness should come via a good squeeze of lime juice, but how wrong I was.

SERVES 4

TAKES 35 mins, plus marinating

4 skinless, boneless chicken thighs, sliced into thin strips

1½ tbsp jerk seasoning

leaves from a few sprigs of soft summer thyme, plus extra to serve

3 tsp groundnut oil, plus extra to drizzle

10 spring onions (scallions), finely sliced and white and green parts separated

2 Scotch bonnet chillies, finely sliced (discard the seeds to keep the heat down, if wished)

1.2 litres (5 cups) good chicken stock

1 corn on the cob

½ green (bell) pepper, diced

½ red (bell) pepper, diced

1 x 400g (14oz) can red kidney beans, drained and rinsed

125g (4½oz) diced fresh pineapple

salt and freshly ground black pepper

Put the chicken in a bowl with the jerk seasoning, thyme, a pinch of salt and 2 teaspoons of oil. Let marinate for 2–3 hours, or overnight in the fridge.

Heat the remaining oil in a large saucepan. Fry the chicken over high until browned and caramelizing on the outside. Reduce the heat to medium, add the spring onion whites and chillies and cook until softened. Add the stock and let it bubble away for a few minutes until the chicken is cooked through.

Meanwhile, heat a grill (broiler) to its highest setting. Drizzle the corn cob with a little oil and grill, turning frequently, until it is charring all over (you still want some yellow). You could also do this with a chef's blowtorch. Allow the cob to cool a little, then use a sharp knife to slice off the kernels.

Add the corn to the soup, along with the peppers and kidney beans, and cook for 2–3 minutes, until the peppers are just softening (but you still have a fresh crunch) and the beans are heated through. Add the pineapple and spring onion greens, season well with salt and pepper and cook for a few more seconds, just until they are heated through.

Ladle into bowls and sprinkle with a little more thyme to serve.

Pink Peppercorns with
Prawn & Pernod Broth

This one's a light starter on a balmy summer's eve when you're in the relaxed, chilled-glass-of-Sauvignon-at-arm's-reach-induced mindset to appreciate the subtle interplay between the shellfish and anise flavours, plus a little spicy hit when you bite on an aromatic pink peppercorn. If you make the Pepper & Tomato Chunky Creole Fish Stew on page 80, keep the prawn heads and shells and use them to intensify this stock – you can just pop them in the freezer until needed.

 SERVES 4

 TAKES 45 mins

For the stock
heads and shells from the prawns (shrimp) – see below
1 onion, peeled and quartered
1 large leek, chopped into chunks
1 large carrot, chopped into chunks
1 celery stick, chopped into chunks
a few black peppercorns

For the broth
6 spring onions (scallions), finely sliced on a deep angle, white and green parts separated
2 bulbs baby fennel, shredded very finely on a mandoline
2 tsp pink peppercorns
400g (14oz) large fresh prawns (shrimp) in their shells
2 tbsp Pernod
a large handful of Japanese greens (such as baby purple pak choi)
sea salt

To make the stock, peel the prawns and put the heads and shells in a large saucepan. Add all the remaining ingredients along with 1.4 litres (6 cups) of water. Cover and bring to a simmer over a medium heat, skimming off any foam or scum from the top. As soon as the liquid is simmering, remove the lid and lower the heat to medium–low. Allow to simmer gently, uncovered, for about 30 minutes. Allow the stock to cool a little, then strain and return to a clean saucepan.

Add the spring onion whites, fennel and pink peppercorns to the stock and simmer for 4–5 minutes, until the fennel is tender. Taste and season the stock well with salt – it will take quite a lot – but you shouldn't need any more pepper.

Add the prawns to the stock along with the spring onion greens and the Pernod and cook for 3 minutes more, or until the prawns are just cooked and their flesh is opaque.

Sprinkle a few Japanese leaves into the bottom of 4 shallow bowls. Ladle the broth between the bowls, dividing the prawns evenly between them, then serve.

Whipped Lemon Ricotta with
Sorrel & Avocado Soup

In my first home with a garden, the first thing I did was plant several sorrel plants. Relatively unknown, sorrel is a wonderful tangy, citrussy herb. Cooking impairs it: raw, it keeps its vibrant colour and sharp bite. Here, I've balanced it with creamy avocado and velvety whipped ricotta. There are a lot of raw green soups that taste just that bit too, well, 'green'. I'm happy to say this isn't one of them.

 SERVES 4

 TAKES 10 mins

For the whipped lemon ricotta
150g (5½oz) ricotta cheese
  (or vegetarian alternative)
finely grated zest of 1 small lemon
salt and freshly ground black pepper

For the soup
100g (3½oz) sorrel leaves
200g (7oz) peeled and roughly diced
  avocado flesh (about 1 smallish
  avocado)
250g (9oz) cucumber, roughly
  chopped into chunks
450ml (2 cups) coconut water, ice cold

Put the ricotta in a mixing bowl with the lemon zest and beat it with an electric hand whisk until well combined. Season with a little salt and pepper and set aside.

Put all the soup ingredients in a high-speed blender and blitz until smooth. Season with salt and pepper.

Pour the soup into small bowls or wide cups (you only need small servings of this), top with a spoonful of the lemon ricotta and serve immediately.

Sweet & Smoky Tomato,
Chorizo & Squid Soup

There are two ways to cook squid – quick and blisteringly hot, or gentle and drawn-out. Here, I've opted for the latter, and it's so easy: once it's bubbling happily, you can walk away and let it do its thing, safe in the knowledge that the squid will be deliciously tender in the end.

 SERVES 4

 TAKES 1 hr 30 mins

2 tbsp olive oil, plus extra for drizzling
160g (5½oz) chorizo, diced
1 large onion, finely diced
3 garlic cloves, finely chopped
1 tbsp sweet smoked paprika
   (pimentón dulce)
600ml (2½ cups) light fish stock
   (or 1 jelly stock pot in 600ml/
   2½ cups hot water)
500ml (2 cups) passata
   (strained tomatoes)
1 x 400g (14oz) can chopped
   tomatoes
leaves from 2 bushy thyme sprigs
1 squid tube, cleaned and thinly sliced
   into rings (include the tentacles,
   too, sliced up)
2 large red (bell) peppers, halved and
   deseeded
salt and freshly ground black pepper
rocket (arugula), to serve

Preheat the oven to 190°C fan/375°F/Gas 5.

Add oil to a large saucepan set over a high heat then add the chorizo. Cook until it's browned and beginning to release its oils. Reduce the heat to low–medium and add the onion, garlic and a pinch of salt. Cook for 6 minutes, or until the onions are really softening. Add the smoked paprika and cook for a couple more minutes, then add the stock, passata, tomatoes, thyme and the squid. Put a lid on the pan and leave to bubble gently for about 1¼ hours, or until the squid is really tender.

Meanwhile, put the peppers on a baking sheet and drizzle with olive oil. Roast for 25–30 minutes until soft and the skins are beginning to char. Use tongs to immediately remove the peppers to a bowl and cover with cling film (plastic wrap) or a plate. Leave them for 15 minutes or so – the trapped steam will help the skins come off. Once cool enough to handle, peel off and discard the skins and thinly slice the peppers.

Once the soup has had its time, tip in the peppers, along with any juices that may have collected in the bottom of the bowl. Season well with salt and pepper and serve in warmed bowls with a small handful of rocket on the top of each.

Fresh Asparagus Soup

Asparagus can easily be overpowered, so here I suggest a delicate homemade stock. You can sub it out for shop-bought, if you must, but you risk the artificial tang of processed bouillon bullying its way through the subtle asparagus. The only – gentle – sharpness should be from the contrasting colourful sweet radish pickles.

 SERVES 4

 TAKES 1 hr 15 mins

2 tbsp olive oil
1 onion, diced
1 leek, sliced
2 carrots, peeled and sliced
1 fennel bulb, diced
1 celery stick, sliced
100g (3½oz) button mushrooms
1 bay leaf
a bunch of parsley stalks
a few black peppercorns
2 garlic cloves, peeled and lightly
    bashed with the side of a knife
150g (5½oz) peeled and diced potato
500g (1lb 2oz) trimmed asparagus
4 tbsp crème fraîche, plus 4 tsp
salt and freshly ground black pepper
shelled hemp seeds, to serve

Heat the oil in a large saucepan and add the onion, leek, carrots, fennel and celery. Sauté for 10 minutes, or until the vegetables are starting to colour.

Add 1.2 litres (5 cups) of water, the mushrooms, bay leaf, parsley, peppercorns and garlic. Bring to a simmer and leave for 30 minutes.

To prepare the radishes (see ingredients overleaf), very thinly slice them, then place in a bowl. In a jug, combine the vinegar and honey and stir until the honey has dissolved. Pour over the radishes and leave to pickle for 30 minutes (any longer and they'll go floppy), stirring occasionally. Drain well then set aside.

Once the 30 minutes is up, strain the stock into a clean saucepan. Use a spoon to push the stock through the sieve, mashing the veg a little to get out all the liquid. Add the potato and bring to a simmer over a medium heat. Cover and cook for 12 minutes, until the potato is almost cooked. Add the asparagus, re-cover and cook for 4–5 minutes, until the asparagus is just tender.

ingredients and method continue overleaf…

Fresh Asparagus Soup

continued...

For the pickled radishes

100g (3½oz) radishes

3 tbsp white rice vinegar

2 tbsp clear honey

Transfer the soup to a liquidizer and blend until smooth. Add the crème fraîche and blitz again. Taste and season with salt and black pepper.

Ladle the soup into 4 warmed bowls. Top with a little crème fraîche, a few radishes and some hemp seeds.

Spring Greens & Peas with
Cidery Ham Hock Soup

We know how much pork and apple love a liaison, so it wasn't too far a stretch to switch a bit of the stock for some cider. The cider adds a slight sweetness to the already salty ham, which makes this pretty irresistible. If a portion or two does make it through to the next day, it will probably have set solid because of the gelatine in the stock. Just reheat it, adding a splash of water if need be, and it will be as good as new, if not improved by the flavours having had a night to get better acquainted.

 SERVES 4–6

 TAKES 3 hrs, plus soaking

For the ham and stock
1.2kg (2½lb) smoked ham hock
4 whole cloves
1 large onion, halved
2 large carrots, roughly chopped
1 large leek, chopped into chunks
2 celery sticks, chopped
a few black peppercorns
a bouquet garni
mustard, to serve

Soak the ham hock for 6–8 hours, changing the water every 2 hours to get rid of any excess salt.

Stick the cloves into the onion and add to a large pan with the remaining stock ingredients. Add the ham hock and just cover with water (no more than 2 litres/8 cups). Cover and bring to the boil over a medium heat. Skim the surface of the stock, then turn the heat down to low–medium and simmer for 2 hours. Remove the lid towards the end of cooking, but make sure the meat is still submerged in liquid so it doesn't dry out.

Strain the stock into a clean pan, discarding the veg and reserving the ham. Cook down until you have reduced it to 1.2 litres (5 cups) of stock. Meanwhile, once the ham is cool enough to handle, shred the meat from the bone, cover and set aside.

Heat the oil and butter in a large saucepan and add the onion, celery and garlic. Cook over a low heat for 10 minutes, until well softened. Add the cider and turn up the heat. Cook for 10 more minutes, or until the cider has reduced by half.

ingredients and method continue overleaf...

Cidery Ham Hock Soup

continued...

For the soup
1 tbsp light olive oil
1 tbsp butter
1 onion, finely diced
1 celery stick, finely sliced
1 garlic clove, crushed
500ml (2 cups) artisan (hard) cider
200g (1½ cups) frozen peas, thawed
150g (3 cups) shredded spring greens
a small handful each of mint leaves
    and flat-leaf parsley, chopped
salt and freshly ground black pepper

Add the reduced stock and bring to the boil. Add the peas, spring greens and the meat and cook for a minute or so. Taste and season with salt, if needed, and plenty of black pepper.

Stir in the herbs just before serving, ladle into bowls and serve, with mustard on the side, if you like.

Udon, Edamame & Shiitake with
Salmon & Miso Broth

All of the usual indicators of fullness seem to abandon me when I make this. I guess it's the miso that should be thanked – that moreish, umami master encouraging furtive slurps directly from the ladle each time the pan is casually, yet repeatedly, passed. For that very reason, miso is not something to be compromised on here; if the supermarket doesn't have the sweet white variety, go to a health food store.

SERVES 4

TAKES 15 mins

2 tbsp vegetable oil

5cm (2in) piece fresh ginger, peeled and grated

2 garlic cloves, crushed

120g (4oz) shiitake mushrooms, sliced

1.2 litres (5 cups) hot good-quality fish stock (use prepared stock or jelly stock pots if not making your own, not cubes)

1 tbsp mirin

100g (3½oz) dried brown rice udon noodles

150g (5½oz) frozen shelled edamame

2 heads of pak choi (bok choy), sliced, white and green parts separated

6 spring onions (scallions), sliced and white and green parts separated

4 tbsp sweet white miso paste

350g (12oz) salmon fillet, skinned and cut into 2cm (¾in) dice

sea salt (optional)

Heat the oil in a large pan over a low heat and fry the ginger and garlic gently for 3–4 minutes until smelling fragrant. Add the mushrooms and cook for another minute or so until just wilted.

Add the stock to the pan, then stir in the mirin. Add the noodles, turn up the heat to medium–high and bring to the boil. Add the edamame, and bring back to the boil. Once boiling again, add the white parts of the pak choi and spring onions and return the heat to boiling. Cook for a few minutes until the liquid is hot and bubbling again.

Add the miso and stir in, then check the noodles – they should be very close to being perfectly cooked before you add anything else. Add the salmon pieces and pak choi greens and cook for 1–2 minutes maximum, until the salmon is just cooked and the greens are wilted. Season with salt, if needed.

Spoon the broth between 4 warmed bowls and sprinkle with the spring onion greens to serve.

Olive Oil Croutes with
Med Veg Soup

Pomegranate molasses is so alluring on the supermarket shelf... but you get it home and that promising bottle soon gets pushed to the back of the cupboard, not to see the cold light of day for months. This recipe is a great way to get inspired to use it: it can add depth and a wonderful sweet and sour element to a pan of almost anything.

 SERVES 4

 TAKES 45 mins

1 large aubergine (eggplant), diced
1 courgette (zucchini), diced (slightly
    smaller than the aubergine)
1 red onion, cut into 6 wedges
    lengthways
2 red (bell) peppers, chopped into
    chunks
4 large garlic cloves, unpeeled
leaves from a few thyme sprigs
4 tbsp olive oil
4 large tomatoes (about 450g/1lb)
1 litre (4 cups) vegetable stock
2 tbsp pomegranate molasses
a large handful of basil leaves, roughly
    ripped, plus extra to serve
salt and freshly ground black pepper

For the croutes
thick slices of crusty bread
extra virgin olive oil, to drizzle, plus
    extra to serve

Preheat the oven to 180°C fan/350°F/Gas 4.

Spread the veg out on a large baking sheet. Add the garlic, sprinkle over the thyme and drizzle with the olive oil. Mix together to coat in the oil. Roast for 30 minutes, stirring halfway, until soft and golden.

Meanwhile, cut a cross in the base of each tomato and place in a heatproof bowl. Pour over boiling water and leave for 20 seconds. Use a slotted spoon to remove. Peel the skins, deseed and dice. Place into a saucepan with the stock and bring to a simmer.

Remove the onions from the baking sheet, discard any papery skin and roughly dice. Squeeze the garlic cloves out of their skins and roughly chop. Tip all the veg into the soup and simmer for 10 minutes: the tomatoes and aubergine will thicken the soup.

Meanwhile, for the croutes, heat a griddle pan until very hot. Drizzle the bread with olive oil and press them onto the hot griddle. Toast for 4 minutes on each side, or until black lines appear.

Add the pomegranate molasses to the soup and season. Stir in the basil just before serving. Ladle into 4 bowls, scatter over a few extra basil leaves and drizzle with olive oil. Serve with croutes on the side.

Makrut Lime, Baby Veg & Coriander
Coconut Fish Soup

For a quick, light lunch, this soup is hard to beat. Gently infused with lime and sweet coconut, it somehow manages to work as a summer refresher or a winter warmer, and can be on the table in less than half an hour. To bulk it out a bit, add some rice noodles towards the end of cooking.

 SERVES 4

 TAKES 30 mins

800ml (3¼ cups) fish stock, preferably homemade
10 fresh makrut lime leaves
5 large slices fresh ginger
3 garlic cloves, whole but bashed
8 spring onions (scallions), greens sliced on the diagonal and whites halved lengthways
½ green chilli, halved lengthways
1 small bunch coriander (cilantro), stalks separated and leaves roughly chopped
1 x 400ml (14oz) can coconut milk
100g (3½oz) baby corn, halved lengthways
50g (2oz) mangetout (snow peas) or sugar snap peas, halved on the diagonal
2 sea bass fillets, chopped into chunks
a squeeze of lime juice
sea salt
lime wedges, to serve

Put the fish stock in a saucepan and add the lime leaves, ginger, garlic, spring onion whites, chilli and coriander stalks. Bring the liquid to a simmer, then simmer for 20 minutes, with the lid on, until the stock is well infused with the flavours.

Strain the stock into a clean pan and add the coconut milk. Bring the liquid up to a simmer again (don't boil once the milk is added) and add the baby corn. Cook for about 3 minutes until it is beginning to soften. Add the mangetout and sea bass and cook for 2–3 minutes more, until the fish is just cooked and all the veg is tender but with a little crisp bite.

Stir in most of the coriander leaves and spring onion greens, then season with a good squeeze of lime juice and a little salt.

Ladle into 4 warmed bowls and serve topped with the reserved coriander and spring onion greens, and with lime wedges on the side for squeezing over.

Orange & Oregano with
Black Olive Borscht

The inclusions (and omissions) to this dish give it an interesting twist, taking it from Kyiv by way of Kefalonia. The lighter flavours present the challenge of getting the balance perfectly right – no single flavour should dominate. Master that and you will be rewarded.

 SERVES 4

 TAKES 1 hr 30 mins

500g (1lb 2oz) beetroot (beets) (try and get them all roughly the same size so they cook evenly – I used 5, about 100g/3½oz each)
2 tbsp olive oil
1 onion, finely diced
1 carrot, peeled and finely diced
1 celery stick, finely diced
1 large garlic clove, finely chopped
1.2 litres (5 cups) good beef stock, preferably homemade
juice of ½ orange (about 3 tbsp), freshly squeezed
1 tsp finely grated orange zest
2 tbsp finely chopped fresh oregano, plus optional extra to serve
30g (1oz) black olives, finely sliced
sea salt and freshly ground black pepper

Preheat the oven to 180°C fan/350°F/Gas 4.

Wrap the beetroot in kitchen foil together and place on a baking sheet. Bake for 1 hour, or until tender. Once cooked, rub the skins away – they should slip off easily – and grate the beetroot, discarding the stalks.

Heat the oil in a large saucepan set over a low heat and add the onion, carrot, celery and garlic. Sauté very gently for about 15 minutes, or until everything is well softened and the onion is translucent.

Add the stock and bring to the boil, then lower the heat so the liquid is just simmering and add the orange juice and zest, oregano, olives and grated beetroot. Heat through for a few minutes until everything is warm, then season really well with salt and pepper.

Ladle into bowls and top with a sprinkle more oregano to serve, if you like.

Kelp, Shiitake & Sesame

Carrot & Tofu Broth

Like any good stock, this takes time to make, so it's worth doubling up and making a big batch. It's restorative and has an intense savouriness, thanks to the umami-rich seaweed, miso and shiitake mushrooms. If you only have brown miso, just add 1 tablespoonful.

 SERVES 4

 TAKES 1 hr 20 mins

For the broth
1 red (bell) pepper, roughly chopped
3 large carrots, sliced
1 large leek, sliced
1 large onion, roughly sliced
1 celery stick, sliced
3 garlic cloves, cut in half
a drizzle of light olive oil
5 kelp knots
8g (¼oz) dried shiitake mushrooms
a bunch of parsley stalks
6 black peppercorns
2 tbsp white miso paste (see intro)
sea salt

To serve
2 tbsp sesame seeds
1 tbsp olive oil
225g (8oz) firm smoked tofu, diced
6 long skinny carrots, any colours
toasted sesame oil, to drizzle

Preheat the oven to 190°C fan/375°F/Gas 5.

Put the pepper, carrots, leek, onion, celery and garlic cloves on a large baking sheet. Drizzle with oil then mix to lightly coat the vegetables. Put in the oven and bake for about 40 minutes, stirring halfway through, until wilted and caramelizing.

Tip the cooked veg into a saucepan. Cover with 1.2 litres (5 cups) of cold water. Add the kelp, shiitake, parsley and peppercorns. Bring to the boil, then reduce the heat and simmer gently for 30 minutes. Strain the stock into a clean pan. Stir in the miso and season with salt. Keep warm over a low heat.

Heat a large frying pan over a medium heat and add the sesame seeds. Toast for 3 minutes or so, stirring, until turning golden and smelling toasty. Immediately tip on to a plate.

Add the oil to the same frying pan and fry the tofu for about 5 minutes until golden on all sides.

Ribbon the carrots with a vegetable peeler and divide between 4 shallow bowls. Pour in the broth (the carrots will wilt and cook a little). Divide the tofu evenly between the bowls. Sprinkle with toasted sesame seeds and drizzle with sesame oil.

Rhubarb, Mint & Pistachio
Springtime Broth

Tending your vegetable patch may be a ridiculously relaxing way to spend a Sunday afternoon, but when the same old vegetables appear at every meal, tedium is not far behind. Finding new ways to use the harvest is half the fun. If you have a crop of rhubarb and you can't face another crumble, try this healthful veggie broth, where it breaks down to provide a fresh, fruity background flavour.

SERVES 4

TAKES 25 mins

40g (3 tbsp) butter

2 stems tender young rhubarb, sliced about 4mm (⅛in) thick

5 spring onions (scallions), sliced and white and green parts separated

1.2 litres (5 cups) vegetable stock

2 tsp cornflour (cornstarch)

a small handful of sugar snap peas

70g (2½oz) asparagus tips

70g (2½oz) purple sprouting or long-stem broccoli

70g (2½oz) baby broad (fava) beans

70g (2½oz) peas (defrosted if frozen)

3 tbsp snipped chives

3 tbsp finely chopped parsley

salt and freshly ground black pepper

For the mint & pistachio pesto

25g (1oz) mint leaves

15g (½oz) pistachio nuts

3–4 tbsp extra virgin olive oil

1 small garlic clove, chopped

Put the butter in a large saucepan set over a low heat and let it melt. Add the rhubarb and cook gently for about 5 minutes until it's starting to soften. Add the spring onion whites and cook for another minute, then add the stock and bring the liquid up to the boil.

Mix the cornflour with a little water in a small bowl. Add it to the pan and cook for a few minutes until the broth starts to thicken a little.

Meanwhile, put all the ingredients for the pesto in a mini chopper or the small bowl of a food processor and blitz until smooth. Season well with salt and pepper and set aside.

Thickly slice the sugar snaps, then slice the asparagus tips on the diagonal. Slice the broccoli lengthways through the stems if they are thick. Add to the broth and cook for 3 minutes, then add the broad beans, peas and spring onion greens and cook for 1 minute more. Stir in the herbs, then taste and season well with salt and pepper.

Serve the soup immediately (so the veg are still a little crisp and still bright green), in warmed shallow bowls with a dollop of pesto on top.

Crab, Chilli & Lime Dumplings in
Thai Broth

Here, rice paper discs are far quicker than making a classic gyoza-esque dumpling dough. These may not be the most elegant of dumplings but rolling them up creates layers, which add strength to the fine rice paper and keep all that zingy filling contained once buoyed in the hot broth.

SERVES 4

TAKES 30 mins

1.2 litres (5 cups) chicken stock
½ red chilli, plus extra sliced chilli to serve (optional)
2 lemongrass stalks
4 thick slices fresh ginger
1 tbsp Thai fish sauce
a squeeze of lime juice
a handful of Thai basil leaves
sea salt
lime wedges, to serve

For the dumplings
250g (9oz) fresh crab meat (all white meat or half brown, half white)
2 spring onions (scallions), very finely chopped
½ red chilli, very finely chopped
finely grated zest of ½ lime
a small handful of coriander (cilantro) leaves, chopped
16 rice paper wrappers (I use 16cm/6¼in discs)

Put the stock in a saucepan and add the chilli, lemongrass and ginger. Cover the pan and bring to a simmer. Simmer for 20 minutes or so, until the flavours have had a chance to infuse the stock.

Meanwhile, make the dumpling fillings. Combine the crab, spring onions, chilli, lime zest and coriander in a bowl and season with salt.

Fill a shallow bowl with warm water. Take a rice paper disc, dip it in the water for a few seconds, then lay on a board. Spoon a heaped teaspoon of the crab mixture onto one side of the disc, and roll up, tucking in the sides as you go, as you would a spring roll. Repeat to roll 16 dumplings.

Strain the stock, discarding the aromatics, and return to the pan. Add the fish sauce and a squeeze of lime juice. Season to taste – the fish sauce is very salty so you may not need to add any extra salt.

Add the dumplings to the pan, a few at a time, and cook for up to 30 seconds to warm the crab through. Transfer to 4 shallow bowls. Divide the broth between the bowls and add several Thai basil leaves to each bowl. Sprinkle with extra chilli, if using, and serve with lime wedges for squeezing.

Lemongrass & Samphire
Mussel Broth

This is a shameless twist on moules marinières, leaving out the conventional aromatics of thyme and bay and replacing them, perhaps brazenly, with a lemongrass stalk or two. As there is more cooking liquor to make this more soupy, a good fish stock is important; make it fresh, following my recipe on page 12, if you can.

SERVES 4

TAKES 20 mins

2 tbsp butter
1 tbsp olive oil
3 large echalion shallots, finely sliced
2 lemongrass stalks, very finely sliced
(try and get it into shavings with a
very sharp knife)
2 garlic cloves, finely chopped
1.2kg (2½lb) mussels
200ml (generous ¾ cup) white wine
1.4 litres (6 cups) good fish stock
100g (3½oz) samphire
a small handful of flat-leaf parsley
leaves, roughly chopped
sea salt and freshly ground black
pepper
crusty bread, to serve

Heat the butter and oil in a large saucepan set over a low heat and add the shallots, lemongrass and garlic. Cook very gently for about 10 minutes, or until everything is well softened.

While the onions are softening, prepare the mussels. Wash and de-beard them. Discard any that are open and that don't close when given a sharp tap on the shell with your knife, as these may be dead.

Add the wine to the pan, turn up the heat to medium and let it reduce until the liquid has almost all gone. Add the stock to the pan, put the lid on and bring it to the boil, then reduce the heat so that the liquid is just simmering and add the mussels and the samphire. Cook for 3–4 minutes, until the mussels are cooked and have all opened and the samphire is tender.

Taste the broth and season with salt and pepper, then stir in the parsley just before serving. Ladle into shallow bowls, picking out and discarding any mussels that have not opened as you go, and serve with crusty bread.

Smoked Salmon & Dill Soured Cream with
Courgette Soup

I've left the caraway seeds whole here, so that even once blended, you'll still get little hits of that lovely aniseedy fennel-like flavour, but you could grind the seeds more finely in a pestle and mortar first, if you prefer. Ever the Scandiphile, I've taken this north and added salmon and dill to the caraway, though if you want to keep it vegetarian, just leave out the salmon.

 SERVES 4

 TAKES 25 mins

2 tbsp olive oil
1 onion, diced
1 garlic clove, finely chopped
1¼ tsp caraway seeds
800g (1lb 12oz) courgettes
  (zucchini), sliced
800ml (3¼ cups) vegetable stock
50g (⅓ cup) easy-cook rice
3 tbsp soured cream
a small handful of chives,
  plus extra to serve
a small handful of dill fronds
sea salt and freshly ground
  black pepper

To serve
4 tbsp soured cream
2 tbsp chopped dill
80g (3oz) smoked salmon, sliced
  into thin strips

Heat the oil in a large saucepan set over a low heat and sauté the onion, garlic and caraway seeds for 10 minutes, until the onion is soft and translucent. Add the courgettes, stock and rice and cook for 10–12 minutes, or until the rice is tender and the courgettes are softened.

Meanwhile, combine the soured cream and dill for serving and pop in the fridge until needed.

Once it's had its time, transfer the soup to a blender, add the 3 tablespoons of soured cream and blitz until smooth. Add the herbs and blitz again briefly to just blend them in (it's nice to see flecks of them in the soup). Tip the soup back into the cleaned pan and season to taste with salt and pepper.

Ladle the soup into warmed bowls and top each serving with a spoonful of the dill soured cream. Finish with a scattering of salmon ribbons, a few snipped chives and a good grind of coarse black pepper.

Feta, Mint & Toasted Seeds with
Watermelon Gazpacho

Watermelon seeds are having something of a moment. I'm not one for superfood magic bullets: the seeds' inclusion here is simply in the spirit of mottainai – waste not, want not. *You don't want the black bits making your soup speckly or getting between your teeth when you eat it, so as you're picking them out anyway, they are pretty tasty when roasted and add another interesting texture. Skip them by all means if you can't be bothered.*

SERVES 4

TAKES 25 mins, plus chilling

600g (21oz) prepared watermelon (peeled and diced, black seeds picked out and reserved)

200g (7oz) peeled cucumber, cut into chunks

3 large tomatoes (about 300g/ 10½oz), deseeded and cut into chunks

1 small garlic clove

½ small red onion

3 tbsp olive oil, plus extra to drizzle

½ tbsp sherry vinegar

sea salt and freshly ground black pepper

100g (3½oz) Greek feta cheese, to serve (opt for a vegetarian alternative if necessary)

a small handful of mint leaves, finely shredded, to serve

Put the watermelon, cucumber, tomatoes, garlic, onion, olive oil and sherry vinegar in a liquidizer and blitz to a smooth, thick liquid. Taste and season with salt and pepper. Tip the gazpacho into a bowl or large jug and put in the fridge to chill for at least 2 hours before serving.

Meanwhile, preheat the oven to 180°C fan/350°F/ Gas 4. Dry the seeds that you have picked out of the melon really well with a piece of kitchen paper, then tip them onto a baking sheet. Drizzle with a little olive oil, sprinkle with salt and stir everything together. Pop in the oven to roast for about 10–15 minutes until crisp and toasty smelling.

To serve, give the chilled soup a really good stir and pour into bowls. Top with a crumble of feta and a sprinkling of mint. Finish with a few of the toasted seeds sprinkled over the top.

Korean-inspired
Bibim-Broth

Gochujang, a smoky red chilli paste, and the classic kimchi will give any veg that may have been hanging around in the fridge a new lease of life. Follow the veggie suggestions below, or just add whatever you have to hand. A couple of tips here: a mandoline will speed up the process hugely, and buying your kombu from an east Asian supermarket will cost you far less than buying it from a health food store.

 SERVES 4

 TAKES 15 mins, plus soaking

10g (⅓oz) dried kombu
15g (½oz) dried shiitake mushrooms
200g (7oz) rice vermicelli noodles
4 tbsp kimchi, plus extra to serve (opt for a vegetarian option if necessary)
4 tsp gochujang, plus extra to serve
sea salt

A selection of the below
daikon radish, julienned
carrot, julienned
courgette (zucchini), spiralized or julienned
Chinese (or napa) cabbage, shredded
spinach, wilted
beansprouts
spring onions (scallions), sliced on the diagonal
mangetout (snow peas), sliced on the diagonal

To make the dashi stock, if the kombu is in large sheets, cut it into thick strips. Put it in a saucepan with the dried shiitake and cover with 1.2 litres (5 cups) of cold water. Leave to soak for an hour.

Put the rice noodles in a large bowl and cover with warm water. Leave to soak for about 20 minutes, or until well softened.

Once the kombu and mushrooms have soaked, put the pan over a low–medium heat and bring it up to a simmer slowly. Before it gets to boiling point, remove the pan from the heat and strain the dashi, discarding the kombu and mushrooms. Taste and season the stock with salt.

Divide the softened noodles between 4 bowls. Arrange piles of your chosen vegetables around the bowls, adding a spoonful each of kimchi and gochujang to each bowl, too.

Gently ladle the dashi evenly between the bowls, being careful not to ruin your arrangement, and serve with extra kimchi and gochujang on the side, and with chopsticks and a spoon for eating.

Veggie Noodle
Chicken Soup

In an attempt to keep this a little lighter than the classic Singapore Noodles on which this is based, I have subbed in noodles made from carrot and courgette, for a refreshing, but still ridiculously comforting, take. If you don't have a spiralizer, just use a peeler to shave the carrot and courgette into flatter noodles.

SERVES 4

TAKES 25 mins

2 tbsp light oil, such as sunflower
 or groundnut
1 onion, sliced
2 garlic cloves, finely chopped
3cm (1¼in) piece of fresh ginger,
 finely chopped
1 tbsp medium curry powder
1 large carrot, spiralized into noodles
1 large courgette (zucchini), spiralized
 into noodles
200g (7oz) cooked chicken, shredded
100g (3½oz) small peeled and cooked
 prawns (shrimp)
½ red (bell) pepper, sliced
1 x 225g (8oz) can sliced water
 chestnuts, drained
1.2 litres (5 cups) hot chicken stock
 (preferably homemade)
2 tbsp premium-quality oyster sauce
2 tbsp dark soy sauce
75g (½ cup) frozen peas, defrosted

Get everything chopped, spiralized and ready to go before you begin cooking; it won't take long at all.

Heat the oil in a large saucepan set over a low heat and add the onion, garlic, ginger and curry powder. Sauté them for about 8 minutes until the onion is well softened.

Meanwhile, divide the carrot and courgette noodles between 4 shallow bowls.

Turn up the heat to medium, add the cooked chicken, prawns, pepper and water chestnuts and cook for 3 minutes or so more until the veg is starting to soften.

Add the hot chicken stock to the pan, along with the oyster and soy sauces and the peas. Cook for just a couple of minutes until the peas are tender, but still bright green. You probably won't need seasoning as both sauces are quite salty.

Ladle the soup over the noodles in the bowls and serve.

Black Bean & Chimichurri
Beef Bone Broth

There is something deeply satisfying about creating a delicious dinner out of what would ordinarily be discarded – and if the purported health benefits are true, all the better! Marrow bones should cost you very little from your local butcher. I've given this bone broth a Mendoza makeover and added chimichurri for a flavour boost, along with black beans for ballast.

 SERVES 4

 TAKES 40 mins

2kg (4½lb) beef bones
a drizzle of olive oil
1 onion, halved
1 leek, chopped into chunks
2 carrots, peeled and chopped
2 celery sticks, chopped
2 bay leaves
a few black peppercorns
a bunch of thyme and parsley stalks
1 x 400g (14oz) can black beans,
   drained and rinsed
salt and freshly ground black pepper

For the chimichurri
½ x 25g (1oz) pack flat-leaf parsley
½ x 25g (1oz) pack coriander (cilantro)
½ x 25g (1oz) pack oregano
3 tbsp extra virgin olive oil
½ tsp chilli (red pepper) flakes
1½ tbsp red wine vinegar
2 garlic cloves, finely chopped

Preheat the oven to 190°C fan/375°F/Gas 5.

Put the bones into a large roasting pan and drizzle with a little oil. Roast for 30 minutes, then allow to cool in the pan. (You can skip this step if you don't have time but it does add flavour to the broth.)

Pick the bones out, leaving any fat in the roasting pan, and place in a large saucepan. Add the onion, leek, carrots, celery, bay leaves, peppercorns and herbs and cover with cold water. Bring to the boil, then lower the heat and skim any scum from the surface. Cover the pan with a lid and simmer gently, for 2 hours.

Meanwhile, put all the chimichurri ingredients in a mini chopper or the bowl of a food processor and pulse to combine, leaving plenty of texture. Season to taste.

Strain the stock, discarding the vegetables and bones, into a clean pan. You can use the broth now or cook it down to concentrate the flavour.

When the stock is ready, tip in the beans, then taste and season with salt and black pepper.

Ladle the broth into bowls and top with a drizzle of the chimichurri, to serve.

Ginger Matchsticks &
Silken Broccoli

I've kept this a joyously quick-to-cook soup, not just for convenience but to keep the freshness of flavour. Despite the creaminess provided by the tofu (don't worry – it isn't detectable once blended in), it still has a light lift, and makes a refreshing change from all those broccoli and blue cheese soups.

SERVES 4

TAKES 30 mins

2 tbsp light oil (such as vegetable or sunflower)
6 fat spring onions (scallions), sliced
2 tbsp peeled and finely chopped fresh ginger
1 garlic clove, chopped
800ml (3¼ cups) homemade or light vegetable stock
1½ heads broccoli, finely chopped
150g (5½oz) firm silken tofu
grated zest of ½ lemon, plus a squeeze of juice
sea salt and freshly ground black pepper

For the fiery ginger matchsticks
2cm (¾in) piece of fresh ginger, peeled
cornflour (cornstarch), for dusting
light oil, for shallow frying

Heat the oil in a large saucepan set over a low heat and sauté the spring onions, ginger and garlic for 10 minutes, or until soft.

Meanwhile, for the matchsticks, cut the ginger into fine strips with a sharp knife or julienne peeler. Sprinkle some cornflour onto a plate and toss the ginger matchsticks in it to lightly coat.

Heat some oil in a small frying pan. Scatter in a few ginger strips and fry, stirring regularly, for 1 minute, or until golden brown. Remove with a slotted spoon and drain on a plate lined with kitchen paper. Repeat with the remaining matchsticks. Set aside.

Once the onions are soft, add the stock and bring to the boil. Add the broccoli, cover the pan and cook for 3 minutes until the broccoli is just cooked but still green. There's not much liquid, so push the broccoli down into it and stir everything around a couple of times during cooking. Transfer the soup to a blender and blitz until very smooth. Add the tofu and lemon zest, and season with salt, pepper and a squeeze of lemon juice. Blend again, then taste and adjust the seasoning, if you need to.

Pour the soup into 4 bowls and top each with a little pile of ginger matchsticks, to serve.

Hearty &
Wholesome

Spinach & Split Pea
Curried Paneer Soup

Perky spices, fresh green spinach, cheerfully yellow lentils and cheese fried to golden loveliness – this is a ridiculously sunny soup. It's a sort of cross between a dhal and a saag paneer. I really like it brothy (it makes a contrast to what you'd usually imagine a dhal to be), but if that feels just too bizarre, feel free to stick an immersion blender in before you add the paneer. Just blend enough to thicken it slightly – you want to leave a fair bit of texture.

 SERVES 4

 TAKES 1 hr 5 mins

1 tsp mustard seeds
1 tsp cumin seeds
3 tbsp light olive oil
1 onion, finely diced
2 garlic cloves, finely chopped
1 tsp garam masala
½ tsp ground turmeric
125g (⅔ cup) yellow split peas
1.2 litres (5 cups) vegetable stock
100g (3½oz) paneer cheese, cut
    into 5mm (¼in) dice (opt for a
    vegetarian alternative if necessary)
75g (1⅓ cups) spinach, shredded
a large handful of coriander (cilantro)
    leaves, roughly chopped
a good squeeze of lemon juice
sea salt and freshly ground black
    pepper

Put the mustard and cumin seeds in a large saucepan and dry fry over a low heat for a couple of minutes until they start to pop and smell aromatic. Add 2 tablespoons of the oil along with the onion, garlic, garam masala and turmeric and continue to cook very gently for about 10 minutes until the onion is soft and translucent.

Add the split peas to the pan and stir to coat them in the spicy oil, then add the stock and cover the pan with a lid. Cook gently for about 40 minutes, or until the split peas are completely tender, but not breaking down.

Just before the soup has had its time, heat the remaining tablespoon of oil in a non-stick (this is important, don't try and do it in any old pan) frying pan and set over a high heat. Once hot, add the cubes of paneer and cook, stirring frequently, until they are golden all over. Tip them onto a plate lined with kitchen paper to drain.

Add the paneer, shredded spinach and coriander to the soup pan and stir in. Cook for just 1 minute or so, until the spinach has wilted down. Season with salt and pepper and a good squeeze of lemon juice and serve in warmed bowls.

Parmesan with
Herby Minestrone

There is a reason minestrone is so ubiquitous – it's the very definition of nourishing. You need to cook a big batch or you'll have a fridge full of lonely vegetable halves. It will keep happily, chilled, for a few days (it even gets better after a day or two) and makes a satisfying packed lunch for the office microwave. Don't let the long list of ingredients put you off – they're all cheap, and if you don't already have all the different herbs, a tablespoon of an Italian herb blend will do the trick.

 SERVES 6–8

 TAKES 45 mins

2 tbsp olive oil
100g (3½oz) smoked bacon lardons
1 each of the following: large onion;
   leek; celery stick; large carrot; red
   (bell) pepper; courgette (zucchini)
2 garlic cloves, chopped
2 x 400g (14oz) cans chopped
   tomatoes
1 litre (4¼ cups) chicken or veg stock
1 tbsp tomato purée (paste)
herb mix (1 tsp dried oregano, 1 tsp
   dried thyme, ½ tsp dried rosemary)
125g (4½oz) tiny soup pasta shapes
100g (3½oz) cavolo nero, thick stalk
   removed and shredded
1 x 400g (14oz) can cannellini beans,
   drained and rinsed
25g (1oz) basil, leaves shredded
25g (1oz) oregano, leaves picked and
   roughly chopped
salt and freshly ground black pepper
finely grated Parmesan, to serve

Heat the oil in a large saucepan over a high heat and add the lardons. Fry for a few minutes until turning golden and crispy, then remove to a plate with a slotted spoon, leaving the oil in the pan.

Finely dice the onion, then finely slice the leek and celery. Roughly dice the carrot, pepper and courgette. Turn the heat down to medium–low and add the onion. Cook for 5 minutes or until starting to soften. Add the leek, celery, carrot, red pepper and garlic to the pan and sauté for about 5 more minutes until all the veg is beginning to soften, then add the courgette and chopped tomatoes and stir everything together.

Add the stock, tomato purée and dried herbs, cover the pan and bring the liquid to the boil. Once boiling, turn it down to medium and simmer the soup for 10 minutes. Add the pasta and cavolo nero and cook for 6–7 minutes, or until all the veg is tender and the pasta is cooked.

Add the cannellini beans and half the fresh herbs. Cook just long enough to heat the beans through. Season to taste with plenty of salt and pepper.

Ladle the soup into bowls and serve sprinkled with the remaining herbs and plenty of Parmesan.

Broccoli & Buckwheat Noodles with
Five-spice Duck

This is like a duck pho – the meat finishes cooking to rarest perfection in the hot broth. If you have a free-ish weekend afternoon, try making your own stock by following the meat stock recipe on page 11 and using duck carcasses, but you can get pretty delicious results from the below, too.

SERVES 4

TAKES 25 mins

2 tsp toasted sesame oil
2 large garlic cloves, sliced
2.5cm (1in) piece of fresh ginger,
   peeled and cut into matchsticks
1 small bunch of spring onions
   (scallions), about 8, sliced on the
   diagonal and white and green parts
   separated
2 tbsp dark soy sauce
2 star anise
1 cinnamon stick
1 tsp Sichuan peppercorns, plus
   a little extra to sprinkle
1.5 litres (6 cups) good chicken or
   duck stock
2 duck breasts
2 tsp Chinese 5-spice powder
120g (4½oz) buckwheat noodles
   (100% if you can find them)
160g (5½oz) Tenderstem broccoli
sea salt

Heat the oil gently in a large saucepan and add the garlic and ginger. Cook for a few minutes, then add the spring onion whites, soy sauce, star anise, cinnamon and Sichuan pepper and cook for 2 more minutes. Add the stock and let the pan bubble away gently while you sort out the duck.

Season the duck breasts with salt, then rub with the 5-spice, all over. Place them in a cold non-stick frying pan, skin side down, and turn the heat up to medium–high. Once the pan is hot, cook for about 6–7 minutes, turning them over two-thirds of the way through, until the fat has rendered out and they are golden and browned on the outside (they will still be a little raw in the middle). Remove from the pan and leave to rest on a chopping board.

Add the noodles to the soup and cook for 3 minutes. Add the broccoli and cook for another 3 minutes, or until the noodles are cooked and the broccoli is tender but still has a bit of bite. Taste the soup and add a little salt if needed, but it may not need it as the soy sauce is salty.

Ladle the soup into bowls. Slice the duck very thinly with a sharp knife and share between the bowls. Finish with a sprinkle of spring onion greens and a little more Sichuan pepper.

Sweet Potato, Shallots & Kale with
Turkey Meatball Soup

There's a bit of groundwork to be done here, but it's worth the effort. If you want to cut corners, you could use cut-up sausages instead of making the meatballs, but it won't be as healthy as using minced turkey, or probably as tasty.

SERVES 4

TAKES 1 hr, plus chilling

For the meatballs
1 tbsp olive oil
1 small red onion, finely diced
1 large garlic clove, crushed
250g (9oz) ground turkey thighs
2 tsp sage leaves
2 tsp rosemary needles
50g (1 cup) fresh brown breadcrumbs
1 egg
½ tsp each of ground allspice, sea salt
   flakes and black pepper
plain (all-purpose) flour, to dust

To make the meatballs, heat the oil in a small frying pan over a low heat. Sauté the onion and garlic gently for 8–10 minutes until really softened. Then turn off the heat and leave to cool in the pan.

Tip the minced turkey into a mixing bowl and add the cooled onion and the remaining meatball ingredients. Using your hands, massage the mixture together until really well combined. Divide into 20 rough balls, place on a plate and cover with cling film (plastic wrap). Chill in the fridge for an hour or so (or longer – you can do this well in advance). Once cold the meatballs will be easier to shape into neater balls, and you can use a dusting of flour on your hands to help, too.

ingredients and method continue overleaf...

Turkey Meatball Soup

continued...

For the soup

200g (7oz) small shallots

2 tbsp olive oil

1 large sweet potato, peeled

1.25 litres (5 cups) chicken stock

leaves from 3 thyme sprigs

100g (3½oz) kale, tough stalks
    removed, roughly torn

1 tbsp Worcestershire sauce

2 tsp wholegrain mustard

For the soup (see ingredients overleaf), finely dice the shallots. Heat the oil in a frying pan set over a medium heat, then fry them for 6–7 minutes, or until caramelized and turning golden, then tip into a large saucepan, holding the oil back in the frying pan. Turn the heat up to high and let the frying pan get really hot, then add the meatballs and fry, turning frequently, until browned on the outside (you may need to do this in batches). Tip the cooked meatballs into the saucepan too.

Dice the sweet potato. Add the stock, sweet potato and thyme to the saucepan, cover and bring to the boil. Once boiling, turn the heat down and simmer for about 15 minutes, or until the sweet potato is tender. Add the kale, Worcestershire sauce and mustard and cook for another 2–3 minutes until the kale has wilted down.

Taste and season well with salt and black pepper, then ladle into bowls, dividing the meatballs evenly between the bowls.

Cabbage & Mushrooms with
Polish Sausage Soup

The Poles have comfort food pegged, and bigos *(hunter's stew) is everything you could hope for on a wintry day. Polish kabanos sausage has an amazing, distinctive smoky flavour that makes it the star of this soup, which is roughly based on that classic Polish dish.*

SERVES 4

TAKES 1 hr, plus soaking

10g (⅓oz) dried mushrooms
1 tbsp olive oil
125g (4½oz) smoked bacon
   lardons or pancetta
100g (3½oz) kabanos sausage, sliced
1 large onion, finely sliced
150g (2 cups) baby button mushrooms
   (chestnut if possible), quartered
½ tsp caraway seeds
½ small white cabbage, cored
   and finely shredded (about
   150g/5½oz prepared weight)
8 juniper berries, crushed
1 apple, grated (leave the skin on)
1.2 litres (5 cups) beef stock
sea salt and freshly ground
   black pepper

Put the dried mushrooms in a bowl. Cover with 100ml (⅓ cup) of hot water and leave to soak.

Heat the oil in a large saucepan over a high heat and add the lardons. Fry them for a few minutes until they are turning golden and the fat is rendering out, then add the sausages and cook for another couple of minutes.

Turn the heat down to low–medium, add the onion, mushrooms and caraway seeds, and cook for about 8 minutes more until the onions are softening and the mushrooms are picking up some colour. Add the cabbage and juniper berries and cook for a further 5 minutes, until the cabbage is well wilted.

Meanwhile, strain the dried mushrooms, reserving the soaking water, and chop them. Add them to the pan along with the apple. Add the mushroom soaking water too, pouring it in slowly and discarding any gritty-looking liquid at the bottom of the jug. Cook for 1–2 minutes until the liquid has reduced, then add the beef stock.

method continues overleaf...

Polish Sausage Soup

continued...

Turn the heat up to bring the liquid to a boil, then once boiling, turn it back down so that the soup is simmering. Cover the pan and leave to bubble away for 30 minutes, until the cabbage is really soft and all the flavours have got to know each other.

Taste and season with salt and plenty of pepper, then ladle into 4 warmed bowls to serve.

Spinach & Cinnamon with
Chickpeas & Chorizo

Credit must go to Rick Stein for the inspiration for this soup. A long time ago, I was cooked a meal with these flavours from one of his wonderful books; this soup is an homage to that dish, which has stayed with me many years later. I can't remember the recipe in detail, and nor would I wish to plagiarize, but the titular ingredients featured and formed a winning combination.

SERVES 4

TAKES 40 mins

1 tbsp olive oil
125g (4½oz) chorizo, diced
1 large onion, finely sliced
2 garlic cloves, finely chopped
1 bay leaf
1 thyme sprig
1 long, chunky cinnamon stick,
   snapped in half
1 litre (4¼ cups) chicken stock
3 large tomatoes (about 350g/12oz in
   total), deseeded and diced
1 x 400g (14oz) can chickpeas
   (garbanzo beans), drained
120g (2½ cups) fresh spinach, roughly
   sliced
sea salt and freshly ground black
   pepper

Heat the oil in a large saucepan set over a high heat and add the chorizo. Cook for about 3 minutes, stirring frequently, until it is beginning to brown and release its oils.

Turn the heat down to low and add the onion, garlic, bay leaf, thyme and cinnamon stick. Cook for about 10 minutes, stirring frequently, until the onion has softened.

Add the stock, pop a lid on the pan and turn up the heat to bring the liquid to a boil. Once boiling, lower the heat to medium to keep the soup at a simmer. Add the tomatoes and chickpeas and allow everything to bubble away for about 10 minutes to infuse the flavours.

Fish out the cinnamon stick halves and bay leaf and discard them. To thicken, transfer a few ladles of the soup (about one-quarter of the total volume) to a food processor and blitz it until smooth. Return the blended soup to the pan. (You could also just blitz briefly with an immersion blender to part-blend, if you prefer a chunkier texture.) Add the spinach and cook for a minute or so until it has wilted down. Taste and season well with salt and pepper, then ladle into warmed bowls to serve.

Barberry & Crispy Onion
Kosheri-ish Soup

I used to believe that if you needed a bowl of something truly comforting and restorative, you had to choose between pasta, or rice, or dhal, or any other complex carb for that matter. And then I discovered kosheri and realized that I was, quite frankly, an amateur. Why choose merely one when you can take a leaf out of the Egyptians' book and stick all three in together?

 SERVES 4–6

 TAKES 45 mins

2 tbsp olive oil
2 onions, finely sliced
3 garlic cloves, finely chopped
1½ tsp ground cinnamon
¾ tsp freshly grated nutmeg
1 tsp ground cumin
30g (2 tbsp) butter (omit if vegan)
75g (⅓ cup) red lentils
40g (¼ cup) white basmati rice
1.3 litres (generous 5 cups) veg stock
30g (1oz) vermicelli/angel hair pasta,
    broken into 2.5cm (1in) pieces
30g (1oz) dried barberries (available
    in most Asian grocers – don't even
    think about skipping them)
zest of ½ small lemon
a good squeeze of lemon juice
salt and freshly ground black pepper
roughly chopped flat-leaf parsley,
    to serve
plenty of crispy fried onions, to serve

Heat the oil in a large saucepan set over a low heat, add the sliced onions, and cook for 10 minutes until softened. Add the garlic and spices and cook for another 10 minutes until the onions are really beginning to caramelize and turn a light golden brown.

Add the butter and let it melt, then add the red lentils and rice and stir them around to coat in the spicy butter. Add the stock, cover the pan with a lid and turn the heat up to high to bring the soup to the boil, then reduce the heat back to medium and simmer for 10 minutes.

Add the pasta and cook for another 7–8 minutes, until it is tender. Turn off the heat and stir in the dried barberries and lemon zest, then taste and season well with salt and black pepper and a good squeeze of lemon juice.

Ladle the soup into warmed bowls and serve with a sprinkling of chopped parsley and tons of crispy fried onions piled on top.

Pepper & Tomato
Creole Fish Stew

The lengthy ingredient list here speaks to the vibrancy of Creole food, but don't let that fool you into thinking this is complicated. This is one-pot cooking at its best – inviting, colourful and relaxed. A welcoming warmth from the cayenne adds authenticity, but the heat shouldn't distract from the delicate taste of the seafood. Don't worry about spending lots on expensive fresh crab – canned will happily disperse itself into the soup base and provide a deep ambient shellfishy flavour.

 SERVES 4–6

 TAKES 35 mins

2 tbsp oil
1 tbsp butter
1 large onion, finely diced
2 celery sticks, finely sliced
3 large garlic cloves, finely chopped
1 red (bell) pepper, diced
1 green (bell) pepper, diced
1 litre (4 cups) fish stock
200ml (¾ cup) passata (strained
   tomatoes)
1 bay leaf
1 tsp each of cayenne pepper, sweet
   smoked paprika, sea salt, dried
   thyme and dried oregano
½ tsp ground black peppercorns
250g (9oz) fresh tomatoes, diced
300g (10½oz) white fish, such as cod,
   cut into 2.5cm (1in) chunks
200g (7oz) large prawns (shrimp),
   shelled weight
1 x 170g (6oz) can lump crab meat
fresh crusty bread, to serve

Heat the oil and butter in a large saucepan over a medium–low heat and sweat the onion and celery for 7–8 minutes until well softened. Add the garlic and peppers and continue to cook for a few minutes more until softened.

Add the stock, passata, bay leaf, spices and dried herbs and cook for about 15 minutes until all the vegetables are tender. Add the tomatoes and cook for about 3 minutes, then add all the fish, prawns and crab and cook for another 3 minutes or until the fish is just cooked.

Ladle the soup into 4 shallow bowls, being careful to divide the lumps of fish and prawns reasonably evenly, and enjoy with fresh crusty bread, to mop up all the juices.

Puy Lentils & Caramelized Red Onion with
Aubergine Soup

This soup certainly isn't going to win any beauty awards — it's too uniformly brown to elicit any genuine delight based on looks alone — but sometimes it really is what's on the inside that counts and, platitudes aside, this is seriously delicious. If you like smoky flavours, it's a great way to prepare aubergines. Try them as a topping for the Barberry & Crispy Onion Kosheri-ish Soup on page 78.

 SERVES 4–6

 TAKES 1 hr 5 mins

2 tbsp olive oil
2 red onions, finely sliced
2 tsp balsamic vinegar
1 large aubergine (eggplant)
2 garlic cloves, finely sliced
120g (⅔ cup) Puy lentils
1.2 litres (5 cups) hot vegetable stock
2 bushy sprigs of thyme
1 rosemary stalk, needles picked and
    finely chopped
1 bay leaf
1 tbsp mushroom ketchup (such as
    Geo Watkins), or more to taste
sea salt and freshly ground
    black pepper

Start with the onions. Heat the oil in a large saucepan and add the onions, balsamic and a good pinch of salt. Cook over a low heat, stirring frequently, until the onions are caramelized and brown. This could take a good 25 minutes, but don't rush it.

While the onions are cooking, put the aubergine over the naked gas hob (stovetop) flame (or you could use a blowtorch or a very hot electric grill/broiler for this) and cook for 10–15 minutes, turning regularly with tongs, until the skin is charred and cracking all over and the flesh feels soft and squidgy. It might make a bit of a mess, but it's easy to wipe up and is worth it for the intense flavour. Once softened, move the aubergine to a plate and leave until cool enough to handle.

Once the onions are cooked, stir in the garlic and lentils and cook for a couple more minutes. Add the stock, along with the thyme, rosemary and bay leaf, cover the pan with a lid and cook for 20 minutes, or until the lentils are tender.

method continues overleaf...

Aubergine Soup

continued...

Meanwhile, remove the skin from the aubergine, removing as much of the charred flakes as possible. Do this over a plate as juices will run out as you do it and you'll want to collect these. Discard the burnt skin and chop the soft flesh into smallish dice.

Add the aubergine to the pan along with any juices that have accumulated on the plate. Add the mushroom ketchup, then taste and season (generously) with salt and pepper, and more mushroom ketchup, if wished.

Ladle into 4 warmed bowls (pulling out the thyme stalks as you come across them) to serve.

Tomato & Fennel Seed with
Lamb Farro Soup

I used to make a lamb ragù based roughly on this, using minced meat instead of shanks, but I see no reason not to loosen it up a bit as lamb, tomato and fennel seeds form a sort of flavour holy trinity. Cooking the shanks long and slow results in an intense base stock that gives the soup a marvellously deep flavour, but you'll need to start it the day before.

 SERVES 6

 TAKES 2 hrs 30 mins

For the stock

2 lamb shanks

1 large onion, halved

1 large carrot, peeled and chopped into chunks

1 large leek, chopped into chunks

2 large celery sticks, chopped into chunks

a bouquet garni made of parsley stalks, thyme sprig and fresh bay leaf

a few black peppercorns

Put all the stock ingredients in a large saucepan and cover with 2 litres (8 cups) of water. Cover with a lid and bring to the boil over a medium heat. Skim any foam from the surface, then lower the heat to low–medium and cook, loosely covered, for 2 hours, skimming occasionally if more foam is gathering on the top.

When the 2 hours is up, allow to cool a little, then strain out the vegetables and meat and reserve the stock. Discard the vegetables. Once cool enough to handle, strip the lamb from the bones, rip or cut it into small pieces and set aside (in the fridge if not using straight away). Measure the stock and, if you need to, reduce it down in a clean saucepan over a medium heat until you have about 1 litre (4¼ cups). Allow to cool completely until set by the natural gelatine in the meat (it's best to make this the day before), then scrape off and discard any fat from the top.

ingredients and method continue overleaf...

Lamb Farro Soup

continued...

For the soup

50g (2oz) can anchovies in oil,
    drained but oil reserved
1 onion, finely sliced
1 celery stick, finely sliced
1 large carrot, finely diced
2 tsp fennel seeds
2 large garlic cloves, crushed
150ml (⅔ cup) red wine
2 x 400g (14oz) cans good-quality
    chopped tomatoes
1 tsp dried oregano
1 tbsp tomato purée (paste)
75g (2½oz) dried farro grain
sea salt and freshly ground
    black pepper

For the soup, put the oil from the can of anchovies into a large saucepan set over a low–medium heat. Add the onion, celery and carrot and cook for about 5 minutes until starting to soften. Add the anchovies, fennel seeds and garlic and cook gently for another 5 minutes or so until everything is smelling aromatic.

Add the red wine and cook until it has reduced to about half its original volume, then add the lamb stock, tomatoes, oregano, tomato purée and farro and cook for 20 minutes, or until the farro is tender but still has a slight bite. Add the shredded lamb to the soup and leave to just heat through. Taste and season well with salt and black pepper, then ladle into warmed bowls and serve.

Brussels Sprouts & Pancetta
Red Rice Soup

Sautéeing the sprouts rather than stewing them in the stock brings out the best of their flavour, which is helped along with smoky pancetta (make a special trip to a good deli for this) and nutty red rice. If you want to recreate a soupy version of your favourite Christmas side, chuck in a few chopped chestnuts or dried cranberries.

SERVES 4

TAKES 50 mins

2 tbsp olive oil

160g (5½oz) best smoky pancetta, rind removed and diced

1 large onion, diced

2 garlic cloves, finely diced

1.4 litres (6 cups) good chicken stock (preferably homemade)

75g (½ cup) camargue red rice

250g (9oz) brussels sprouts, shredded very finely

¾ tsp freshly grated nutmeg

2 tsp mushroom ketchup (such as Geo Watkins)

sea salt and freshly ground black pepper

Heat the oil in a large saucepan set over a high heat and add the pancetta. Fry it for a few minutes until it is turning golden and crispy and the fat has rendered out. Carefully tip most of the fat into a large non-stick frying pan and set that aside.

Lower the heat under the saucepan to low and add the onion and garlic to the pan. Sauté for about 8 minutes until the onions are soft and translucent. Add the chicken stock and rice to the pan and cover with a lid. Raise the heat to high to bring the liquid to the boil, then lower it to medium and leave to simmer for 25–30 minutes, or until the rice is cooked and tender.

Towards the end of the cooking time, heat the reserved oil in the frying pan set over a high heat and add the shredded sprouts. Sauté for about 4 minutes, stirring frequently, until the sprouts are softened and beginning to brown.

Once the rice is tender, add the sprouts to the soup along with the nutmeg, mushroom ketchup, if using, and some seasoning. Taste and adjust the seasoning if needed, then ladle into warmed bowls to serve.

Blackened Spring Onion & Cashew
Freekeh & Soy Soup

Hunches in the kitchen should generally not be ignored – this soup is proof of that. It's a ragtag jumble of ingredients united by a vague feeling that it would somehow be better than the sum of its parts; it was. Serve it with a fork so you can twist the spring onions up against your spoon, spaghetti-style.

SERVES 4

TAKES 35 mins

2 tbsp olive oil, plus extra to drizzle
1 onion, finely diced
1 carrot, finely diced
1 celery stick, finely diced
1 garlic clove, finely chopped
85g (3oz) greenwheat freekeh
75ml (5 tbsp) dark soy sauce
1.2 litres (5 cups) rich chicken or
    vegetable stock
16 large spring onions (scallions)
sea salt and freshly ground black
    pepper
60g (½ cup) roasted, salted cashews,
    roughly chopped, to serve

Heat the oil in a large saucepan set over a low heat. Add the onion, carrot, celery and garlic. Sauté gently for 10 minutes, or until everything is softening. Stir in the freekeh, then add the soy sauce and cook for 2 minutes, or until the liquid has reduced right down. Add the stock and increase the heat to medium–high until the soup is boiling, then lower the heat so the soup is simmering, pop a lid on the pan and leave to cook for 15 minutes or so until the freekeh is tender.

Meanwhile, trim the tops off the spring onions and just trim enough of the bottoms so that you remove the hairy bits, but there's still enough root to keep them together. Slice them in half lengthways and drizzle with a little olive oil. Brush it all over the onions so they are lightly coated.

Preheat a griddle pan until very hot and add half of the spring onions. Cook for a couple of minutes on each side, turning with tongs, until they are starting to go dark brown in places, but there's still plenty of green to be seen. Remove, then repeat with the remaining spring onions.

Season the soup to taste, remembering that the soy sauce is very salty. Ladle into bowls, top with the charred onions and sprinkle with the cashews.

Pearl Barley, Sage & Celariac Soup with
Pig Cheek & Apple

Pig cheeks are the dark meat of the animal – juicy and, in my opinion, much more flavoursome than most other cuts. They are often ground into mince before they make it to supermarket shelves, but you can usually get them from your local butcher if you ask nicely. Cooked slowly until falling-apart tender and teamed with some complementary veggies and herbs, they make a great base for a hearty soup.

 SERVES 4

 TAKES 2 hrs

2 tbsp olive oil

400g (14oz) pigs' cheeks, diced

1 large onion, diced

1 large garlic clove, finely chopped

8 sage leaves, shredded

1.2 litres (5 cups) chicken stock

2 fresh bay leaves

75g (½ cup) pearl barley

½ small celeriac (celery root), peeled and diced (about 250g/9oz prepared weight)

1 large pink-skinned apple, cored and diced (leave the skin on for a bit of colour)

sea salt and freshly ground black pepper

Heat half the oil in a large saucepan set over a high heat. Fry half of the pigs' cheeks until taking on some colour. Transfer the meat to a plate with a slotted spoon, add the remaining oil, and fry the other half of the meat. Remove that from the pan too, then turn the heat down to low.

Add the onion and garlic to the pan (add a tiny splash of the stock if there's not enough oil left to stop them sticking). Cook for 10 minutes until well softened. Add the meat back in (along with any juices that may have collected on the plate) with the sage and stir together, then tip in the stock and add the bay leaves. Put a lid on the pan and increase the heat to bring the liquid to the boil, then lower the heat until it is just simmering and leave to bubble away for 1 hour.

After an hour, add the pearl barley and celeriac and cook for 20 minutes more. Add the apple and cook for a final 5–10 minutes until the vegetables and the pearl barley are tender and the apple is softened, but not breaking down. Taste and season with salt and black pepper.

Ladle the soup into warmed bowls and serve.

Moroccan-spiced Chicken Soup with
Olives & Couscous

I've a particular fondness for this soupy invention, primarily because it has nursed me through the winter's worst sniffles. A sort of loosened-up version of a tagine, the traditional couscous accompaniment is obligingly built in, and it packs in those healing, anti-inflammatory spices so there's plenty going on, flavour-wise; it'll perk up ailing taste buds if nothing else. I'm not claiming to have cracked the cure for the common cold, but perhaps living through one needn't be so miserable after all?

SERVES 4

TAKES 30 mins

a pinch of saffron threads
2 tbsp olive oil
300g (10½oz) skinned and boneless
   chicken thighs, finely sliced
1 large onion, finely diced
2 large garlic cloves, finely chopped
2.5cm (1in) piece of fresh ginger,
   peeled and finely chopped
1½ tsp ground coriander
1 tsp ground cumin
½ tsp ground turmeric
1.2 litres (5 cups) chicken stock
80g (3oz) wholewheat giant couscous
50g (⅓ cup) green olives, sliced
1 small preserved lemon, flesh
   discarded and skin finely chopped
a large handful of flat-leaf parsley
   leaves, roughly chopped
sea salt and freshly ground
   black pepper

Put the saffron in a small bowl and cover with a splash of warm water. Leave to soak.

Heat the oil in a large saucepan set over a high heat and fry the chicken for a few minutes, stirring frequently, until it's beginning to brown. Turn the heat down to low—medium and add the onion, garlic and ginger and cook for about 8 minutes, or until the onion is really soft. Add the ground coriander, cumin and turmeric, stir in, and cook for another 1 minute or so until they are smelling aromatic.

Add the stock, turn the heat up to high and bring the liquid to the boil, then lower the heat to medium so the soup is simmering. Add the saffron and its soaking water, and the couscous, olives and preserved lemon. Pop a lid on the pan and cook for about 8 minutes, or until the couscous is tender.

Season well with salt and pepper and stir in the parsley just before serving.

Tarragon and Pearled Spelt
Wild Mushroom Soup

Punchy wild mushrooms and the liquorice undertones of tarragon make a pretty good flavour match in this autumnal broth, while spelt provides a satisfying bite. This recipe came to me while watching the closing minutes of Phantom Thread, *and while I can't promise a bowl of it will truly tame an artistic temperament, it will have a good go at quietening any early-onset winter blues. Just make sure you're on good terms with your local greengrocer.*

SERVES 4

TAKES 45 mins

15g (½oz) dried porcini mushrooms
1 tbsp walnut or olive oil
1 large red onion, finely sliced
2 garlic cloves, finely sliced
1 tbsp butter
300g (10½oz) wild mushrooms, sliced
1.2 litres (5 cups) good vegetable stock
1 star anise
100g (⅓ cup) pearled spelt
a good splash of madeira wine
a small bunch of flat-leaf parsley, roughly chopped
a small bunch of tarragon, roughly chopped
soft goat's cheese, to serve (optional)
toasted walnuts, roughly chopped, to serve (optional

Put the dried mushrooms in a small bowl and cover with water (about 100ml/⅓ cup). Leave to soak while you ready the other soup bits.

Heat the oil in a large saucepan over a low heat and add the onion and garlic. Cook gently for about 10 minutes until soft and beginning to caramelize. Add the butter to the pan and let it melt, then add the fresh mushrooms and increase the heat slightly to medium. Cook for 5 minutes until the mushrooms are wilted and beginning to take on some colour.

Meanwhile, strain the dried mushrooms, reserving the soaking water, and chop them roughly.

Add the stock, star anise and spelt to the pan, then add the chopped soaked mushrooms along with the soaking water, slowly, discarding any gritty bits at the bottom. Cook for 15–20 minutes until the spelt is cooked but still has a bite.

Add a splash of madeira to the pan and season well with salt and pepper. Stir in the herbs and serve immediately, topped with a crumble of goat's cheese and a sprinkle of walnuts, if wished.

Wintry Roots & Hardy Herb

Chestnut Soup

This is at heart a fancy Scotch broth, minus the lamb. In its place – and also doing a sterling job of standing in for the pearl barley – are sweet, meaty chestnuts. They provide a different but complementary texture and add a flash of creamy richness in what's essentially a peasant-style stew. While their earthiness chimes with the veggies and stops them feeling out of place, they still manage to proffer a pleasing punctuation mark in a bowl of modest roots.

SERVES 4

TAKES 45 mins

2 tbsp rapeseed (canola) or olive oil
1 onion, diced
1 carrot, peeled and diced
1 parsnip, peeled and diced
½ small swede (rutabaga) (about
    200g/7oz), peeled and diced
1 leek, sliced
1 celery stick, sliced
2 garlic cloves, finely chopped
1.2 litres (5 cups) vegetable stock
leaves from a small bunch of thyme
    sprigs, stripped from stalks
needles from a bushy rosemary sprig,
    chopped
about 8 large sage leaves, shredded
2 bay leaves
1 tbsp cornflour (cornstarch)
90g (3oz) pre-cooked, roasted
    chestnuts, roughly diced
½ tsp wholegrain mustard
salt and freshly ground black pepper

Heat the oil in a large saucepan set over a low heat and sauté the onion for 5 minutes. Add the carrot, parsnip, swede, leek, celery and garlic and cook for another 5 minutes. Add the vegetable stock along with all the herbs and bring to the boil. Lower the heat so that the liquid is simmering and cook for 15–20 minutes until the vegetables are almost tender.

Mix the cornflour with a splash of water, then tip this into the pan and cook for another 5 minutes until the soup has thickened a little and the vegetables are perfectly cooked. Stir in the chestnuts and let them heat through for a couple of minutes. Add the mustard, taste and season well with salt and pepper.

Ladle into warmed bowls to serve.

Slow-baked Greek Bean Soup with
Halloumi Croutons

You'll get a generous casserole dish full of this, but if you're going to go to the trouble of soaking, shelling and slow-cooking beans, you may as well make the effort worthwhile. And it's not without its perks – the gentle monotony of peeling beans was surely the world's therapy before we invented life coaches and bubble wrap.

 SERVES 4

 TAKES 3 hrs 30 mins, plus soaking

250g (1⅔ cups) dried butter (lima) beans
2 tbsp olive oil, plus a drizzle for cooking the halloumi
1 large onion, finely diced
3 large garlic cloves, finely chopped
2 x 400g (14oz) cans chopped tomatoes
1 jelly vegetable stock pot
1½ heaped tbsp tomato purée (paste)
20g (¾oz) fresh oregano, leaves roughly chopped, plus extra to serve
½ tsp dark brown sugar
1 tsp sherry vinegar
sea salt and freshly ground black pepper
1 x 250g (9oz) pack of halloumi, cut into 1.5cm (⅝in) cubes (opt for a vegetarian alternative if necessary)

Put the beans in a bowl and cover with cold water. Leave to soak for a day or so, then remove the skins – this should be easy to do – and set aside.

Preheat the oven to 160°C fan/325°F/Gas 3. Heat the oil in a large casserole over a low heat and sauté the onion and garlic for 10 minutes, or until softened and translucent. Add the first tin of tomatoes, then refill the can with water and tip it into the pan. Add the other tin, 2 more cans of water, then add the shelled beans, stock pot, tomato purée and three-quarters of the oregano. Pop the lid on the casserole and bring to the boil.

Place in the oven and bake for 3 hours, stirring once an hour, until the beans are really tender. They will break down into shards but should still be very soft. Remove the pan from the oven and stir in the sugar, sherry vinegar and the remaining oregano. Season really well with salt and pepper.

For the halloumi, heat a drizzle of oil in a non-stick frying pan over a medium heat. Fry the halloumi for 4–5 minutes, turning frequently, until the cubes are soft and picking up colour on all sides.

Ladle the soup into bowls. Top with the halloumi, a grind of black pepper and a few oregano leaves.

Cherry, Juniper & Venison
Beluga Lentil Soup

Many of the soups in this book achieve the coveted high-satisfaction-to-low-effort ratio. But sometimes you want a bit more: the (eponymously) literal caviar of the pulse clan; a deer that you'd like to imagine has spent its days trotting happily through a leafy royal park; a full-bodied red wine of a good vintage and plump, tangy cherries to add a crucial final bite of sweetness.

 SERVES 4

 TAKES 3 hrs

2 tbsp olive oil
300g (10½oz) diced venison shoulder
2 red onions, finely sliced
1 tbsp good-quality balsamic vinegar
10g (⅓oz) dried porcini mushrooms
2 garlic cloves, finely chopped
8 juniper berries, roughly crushed with the side of a knife
200ml (generous ¾ cup) red wine
1.2 litres (5 cups) beef stock
1 bushy sprig of rosemary, needles picked and finely chopped
1 bay leaf
200g (1 cup) cooked beluga lentils (from a can or pouch, or cooked from dried)
100g (⅔ cup) dried cherries
60g (2 cups) shredded cavolo nero or kale
salt and freshly ground black pepper

In a large saucepan set over a very high heat, add half a tablespoon of oil and brown the venison in two batches, adding more oil if needed, then remove to a plate.

Reduce the heat to low and add the remaining oil. Add the onions, vinegar and a pinch of salt. Cook for 25 minutes or until the onions are caramelizing.

Meanwhile, cover the porcini with 100ml (⅓ cup) of hot water and leave for 15 minutes. Strain the liquid into a jug, then roughly chop the mushrooms.

To the onions, add the garlic and juniper berries. Cook for 3 minutes or so, add the wine and reduce until there are a couple of tablespoons of liquid left in the pan. Add the porcini soaking liquor, pouring it in slowly and discarding any gritty-looking liquid at the bottom of the jug. Continue to cook until the liquid has reduced right down. Then, add the stock, the rosemary, the bay leaf, the chopped porcini and the browned venison. Put the lid on and simmer for at least 1 hour over a low heat, or until the meat is very tender.

Add the lentils, cherries and cavolo nero. Cook for a couple of minutes to warm them through. Season to taste, then ladle into warmed bowls to serve.

Oak-smoked Haddock with
Leek & New Potato Soup

Here, the oak-smoked haddock is flavoursome enough that you don't need too much to add a deep smoky fishy flavour to this lighter version of a chowder.

 SERVES 4

 TAKES 30 mins

1 tbsp olive oil
1 tbsp butter
1 large onion, diced
2 leeks, finely sliced
2 garlic cloves, finely chopped
1.2 litres (5 cups) whole milk
½ jelly vegetable stock pot
160g (5½oz) small new potatoes,
    sliced in half (I use the mini ones,
    but if yours are a bit bigger, just
    quarter them)
2 bay leaves
100g (¾ cup) frozen peas
300g (10½oz) oak-smoked
    haddock (in one large piece),
    skinned and boned
a large handful of flat-leaf parsley
    leaves, roughly chopped
zest and juice of 1 lemon
grated nutmeg, to season
salt and freshly ground black pepper

Heat the oil and butter in a large saucepan set over a low heat and sauté the onion, leeks and garlic gently for about 10 minutes or so until everything is well softened.

Add the milk, stock pot, potatoes and bay leaves, put the lid on the pan and increase the heat to medium–high to bring the liquid to a simmer, but don't let it boil. Once simmering, turn down the heat and leave to simmer gently for 15 minutes or so, or until the potatoes are just a couple of minutes off being completely tender.

Add the peas and the fish and cook for about 4 minutes until the fish is just cooked. Remove it with a large slotted spoon or strainer and flake it into pieces. Add it back to the pan, along with the parsley and the lemon zest. Season the soup well with a little salt (if needed – the fish will be quite salty), plenty of black pepper, a little grated nutmeg and a squeeze of lemon juice.

Ladle the soup into warmed bowls to serve.

Pinto Bean &

Goat Mole Soup

While goat's cheese is universally loved, not much of a market exists for the meat in the UK. This is very unjust, as it's a delicious and underrated meat, and especially suited for cooking long and slow like this. My local butcher sells 1kg (2¼lb) bags of mixed goat meat and bones, which make a great base for this soup with a Mexican chocolate–chilli twist.

SERVES 4

TAKES 2 hrs 45 mins

2–3 tbsp olive oil
1kg (2¼lb) mixed goat meat and
    bones
2 onions, 1 halved, 1 diced
1 celery stick, chopped into chunks
1 carrot, chopped into chunks
a bouquet garni made from a bay leaf,
    thyme sprigs and parsley stalks
3 garlic cloves, finely chopped
1½ tbsp ancho chilli paste
½ tsp ground cumin
½ tsp ground cinnamon
2 tsp dried Mexican oregano
1 x 400g (14oz) can chopped
    tomatoes
1½ tbsp cocoa powder
1 x 400g (14oz) can pinto beans,
    drained and rinsed
2 tbsp smooth almond butter
salt and freshly ground black pepper
coriander (cilantro) leaves, to serve

Heat 1 tablespoon of the oil in a large saucepan and brown half the goat meat and bones for a few minutes, until they have picked up some colour. Remove from the pan with tongs, then repeat with the other half and a little more oil, if needed.

Return all the goat to the pan and cover with 1.5 litres (6 cups) of water. Add the halved onion, celery, carrot and bouquet garni. Cover with a lid and bring to the boil, then lower the heat to a gentle simmer. Cook for 2 hours, or until the goat is tender. Strain the stock into a bowl, and shred the goat meat from the bones. Leave the stock to cool, then use a spoon to skim off as much fat as you can. Then put the stock into a clean pan and cook to reduce down to about 1 litre (4 cups).

Meanwhile, heat the remaining tablespoon of oil in the cleaned large saucepan and sauté the diced onion and garlic for about 10 minutes until translucent. Add the chilli paste, cumin, cinnamon and oregano and cook for another couple of minutes. Tip in the tomatoes and stir in the cocoa.

Add the stock to the pan and cook for 15 minutes. Stir in the meat, beans and almond butter, season with salt and pepper, then ladle into 4 warmed bowls. Serve topped with a few coriander leaves.

Creamy &

Comforting

Cheesy Polenta Croutons &
Three Pepper Soup

The various peppers here add three different dimensions to what's actually a pretty simple soup: sweetness from the red (bell) peppers; smokiness from the pimentón and heat from the chillies. I heartily advise adding the chillies by degrees. Roast them all together but blend them in one at a time, tasting in between, and if the last one doesn't quite make it to the liquidizer, who's watching anyway?

SERVES 4

TAKES 50 mins

5 red (bell) peppers, halved
   and deseeded
2–3 red chillies
3 tbsp olive oil
1 onion, diced
1 large carrot, peeled and diced
1 garlic clove, crushed
1 tbsp sweet smoked paprika
   (pimentón dulce)
800ml (3¼ cups) vegetable stock
sea salt and freshly ground black
   pepper
1 quantity Cheesy Polenta Croutons
   (see page 17), to serve (optional)

Preheat the oven to 180°C fan/350°F/Gas 4.

Put the peppers and chillies on a baking sheet and drizzle with 1 tablespoon of the olive oil. Toss to coat, then roast for 25–30 minutes, or until well softened and the skins are just beginning to char.

Meanwhile, heat the remaining oil in a large saucepan set over a low–medium heat and add the onion. Cook until beginning to soften, then add the carrot, garlic and paprika, and continue cooking for about 5 minutes. Add the stock, pop a lid on the pan and bring it to the boil, then lower to a simmer and cook for 10–15 minutes further.

When the peppers are cooked, add them to the pan. If you like it hot, add the chillies here too. (If you want to add them gradually, you can blend them in at the end for less intensity.)

Remove the pan from the heat and blend with a stick blender or transfer to a liquidizer and blitz until smooth. (Add the chillies here if you need to.) Taste and season with salt and black pepper.

Ladle the soup into warmed bowls and top with a few freshly cooked and still hot cheesy croutons. Serve the rest in a bowl on the side.

Garlicky Cauliflower Soup with
Salsa Verde

This may sound like a peculiar combination, but I'd like to make its case anyhow. Cauliflower needs punchy flavours to lift it, and the slightly sour crème fraîche, salty anchovies and fresh herbs cut through any brassica sulphuriness that might be lingering stubbornly.

SERVES 4

TAKES 35 mins

2 tbsp olive oil
1 large onion, diced
3 large garlic cloves, finely chopped
1 large cauliflower, cut into florets
1 litre (4¼ cups) hot vegetable stock
100g (½ cup) half-fat crème fraîche
sea salt and freshly ground black
    pepper

For the salsa verde
½ (25g/1oz) bag basil, finely chopped
½ (25g/1oz) bag flat-leaf parsley,
    finely chopped
½ (25g/1oz) bag mint, finely chopped
4 tbsp extra virgin olive oil
2 tbsp freshly squeezed lemon juice
8 anchovies, finely chopped
1 tbsp drained capers, finely chopped
¼–½ red chilli, deseeded and finely
    diced (optional)

Heat the oil in a large saucepan set over a low–medium heat and add the onion. Sauté for about 8 minutes until softened and translucent. Add the garlic and cauliflower, turn up the heat to medium–high and cook for a further 5 minutes or so until the cauliflower is well coated in the garlicky oil and is beginning to soften. Add the stock and bring to the boil, then lower the heat and simmer, covered, for about 12–15 minutes until the cauliflower is tender.

Meanwhile, make the salsa verde by combining all the ingredients in a small bowl, adding as much red chilli as you like, if using. Season to taste – remembering that the anchovies are salty so you may not need too much salt – and set aside.

Once the cauliflower is tender, remove the pan from the heat and blend with a stick blender or transfer to a liquidizer and blitz until smooth. Stir in the crème fraîche, then season well with salt and pepper.

Serve the soup in warmed bowls with a good dollop of the salsa verde in the middle.

Chilli & Lemon Oil with Za'atar &
Cannellini Bean Soup

Supper can't get much simpler than this. It relies on store-cupboard staples (I know what you're thinking, but za'atar should be in your store cupboard! It costs no more than any other jar of herb mix at the supermarket), so even if there's not much in the fridge, you'll still be able to whip it up. If apathy is at an all-time high, use a store-bought lemon and/or chilli oil.

 SERVES 4

 TAKES 25 mins

2 tbsp olive oil
1 large onion, finely diced
1 celery stick, finely sliced
2 garlic cloves, finely chopped
1–1½ tbsp za'atar, plus extra to
    sprinkle
700ml (3 cups) vegetable stock
2 x 400g (14oz) cans cannellini beans,
    drained and rinsed
a good squeeze of lemon juice
sea salt and freshly ground black
    pepper

For the chilli & lemon oil
1½ tsp chilli (red pepper) flakes
finely grated zest of 1 lemon
3 tbsp extra virgin olive oil

Combine all the ingredients for the chilli & lemon oil in a small bowl and set aside to infuse while you make the soup.

Heat the oil in a large saucepan set over a medium–low heat. Add the onion, celery and garlic and cook for about 10 minutes, stirring frequently, until everything has softened.

Add 1 tablespoon of the za'atar to the pan and cook for 1 minute, then add the vegetable stock and cannellini beans to the saucepan and turn the heat up to bring the liquid to the boil. Lower the heat and simmer for about 5 minutes, until the beans are heated through. Blend with a stick blender, or transfer to a liquidizer and blitz until smooth. Season to taste with salt, pepper and a good squeeze of lemon juice. Taste and if you think it needs more za'atar, go ahead and add the last ½ tablespoon.

Ladle the soup into warmed bowls and drizzle some of the oil over the top. Finish with a little sprinkling of za'atar and serve immediately – this one doesn't benefit from sitting around.

Hazelnut & Star Anise with
Roasted Carrot Soup

*This is exactly what I'd want after a nippy, autumnal walk
– or during, armed with a trusty Thermos. It does seem like a
lot of star anise, but the little stars are extracted before you
blend, so just imbue the soup with a subtle spiciness rather
than launch a full anise assault. If a good loaf of sourdough
will fit into the backpack too, all the better.*

 SERVES 4–6

 TAKES 1 hr 15 mins

4 large carrots (about 750g/1lb 10oz),
 peeled and chopped into chunky
 batons
2 tbsp hazelnut oil, plus extra to
 drizzle
50g (2oz) blanched hazelnuts
2 tbsp light-flavoured oil, such as
 sunflower or rapeseed (canola)
1 onion, diced
1 smallish sweet potato (about
 150g/5½oz), peeled and diced
1 litre (4 cups) vegetable stock
6 star anise
sea salt and freshly ground black
 pepper

Preheat the oven to 190°C fan/375°F/Gas 5. Put
the carrots in a roasting pan and drizzle with the
hazelnut oil. Season with salt and pepper and stir
so that the carrots are fully coated. Pop in the
oven and roast for 30–40 minutes until the carrots
are tender and browning, stirring halfway through.

Meanwhile, tip the hazelnuts onto a baking
sheet and roast, on the shelf under the carrots,
for 5 minutes, until golden. Let them cool, then
roughly chop and set aside.

While the carrots are cooking, heat the oil in a
large saucepan set over a low heat. Sauté the
onion until starting to soften. Add the sweet
potato and cook for another couple of minutes,
then tip in the stock. Add the star anise and
cover with a lid. Increase the heat to high until
the liquid is boiling, then decrease it to medium
and leave the soup to simmer, still covered, for
about 15 minutes, or until the sweet potato and
onion are completely tender. Remove the pan
from the heat.

method continues overleaf...

Roasted Carrot Soup

continued...

Fish out the star anise from the soup and discard (or keep to decorate the bowls). Add the roasted carrots to the pan, then blend with a stick blender or transfer to a liquidizer and blend until smooth (you may need to do this in batches). Return the soup to a clean saucepan and season well with salt and pepper.

Ladle the soup into warmed bowls and sprinkle the roasted hazelnuts over the top of each bowl. Finish with a good drizzle of hazelnut oil and a sprinkling of black pepper to serve. If you're feeling fancy, you could pop one of the star anise on the top of each bowl to decorate as they are very pretty, but do warn people to leave those in the bowl and not bite into them!

Tortilla Croutons with Chipotle
Sweet Potato Soup

While you'd once (not all that long ago) struggle to find wonderful ingredients such as chipotle morita chillies in your local supermarket, they can now be bought on impulse rather than having to be specifically hunted down. If you want actual heat, go for two chillies; for a gentle tingle and a hint of that amazing smoky chipotle flavour, just add the one.

SERVES 4–6

TAKES 45 mins

2 tbsp olive or rapeseed (canola) oil
1 large onion, diced
2 large garlic cloves, finely chopped
½ tsp ground cumin
½ tsp ground cinnamon
1–2 chipotle morita chillies, roughly chopped
800g (1¾lb) sweet potatoes, peeled and diced
1.2 litres (5 cups) vegetable stock
grated zest of 1 lime, plus a good squeeze of the juice
sea salt and freshly ground black pepper
chopped avocado, to serve
coriander (cilantro) leaves, to serve

Preheat the oven to 180°C fan/350°F/Gas 4.

Heat the oil in a large saucepan set over a low heat and cook the onion and garlic with some salt for about 8 minutes, until softening. Stir in the spices and chillies, then add the sweet potato and cook for 2 minutes, stirring to cover it in the spiced oil.

Add the stock, bring to the boil and cover with a lid. Reduce the heat slightly and leave to simmer, for 15 minutes, or until the sweet potato is tender.

Meanwhile, put the tortilla quarters (see ingredients overleaf) on a large baking sheet. Combine the oil and smoked paprika in a small bowl and brush this over the tortillas. Turn them and brush the other sides too, then sprinkle generously with sea salt flakes. Bake for 5–6 minutes, then turn them over and bake for a further 5–6 minutes, until turning crisp and golden. Remove them from the oven and allow to cool (they will continue to crisp up as they cool).

ingredients and method continue overleaf...

Sweet Potato Soup

continued...

For the tortilla croutons

2 tortillas, cut into quarters

1 tbsp olive oil

1 tsp sweet smoked paprika (pimentón dulce)

a good sprinkling of sea salt flakes

Once the sweet potato is cooked, blend the soup with a stick blender or transfer to a liquidizer and blitz until smooth. Add the lime zest and juice, season to taste and blitz again to combine.

Ladle the soup into warmed bowls and top with the avocado. Snap the tortillas into shards and scatter a few over the top, serving any extra in a bowl. Finally, sprinkle with coriander and serve.

Toasted Almond Sprinkle with
Fennel & Vanilla Soup

Many ready-made almond milks are less than 2.5 per cent nuts. Not being especially keen to promote a lunch that's packed with preservatives, gums, etc., I propose here making your own – it does admittedly require some forward thinking, but what you get is a much creamier, more nutritious milk and a subsequently far superior soup.

 SERVES 4

 TAKES 45 mins

270g (2 cups) whole blanched almonds, soaked in 800ml (3¼ cups) water overnight, plus 30g (2 tbsp) for the topping, sliced thickly
1 tbsp olive oil
1 onion, diced
2 large fennel bulbs, diced (reserve the fronds)
1 large garlic clove, finely chopped
250ml (1 cup) light vegetable stock (preferably homemade)
1 small potato, peeled and diced
¼–½ tsp vanilla bean paste
sea salt and freshly ground black pepper

Tip the soaked almonds into a blender and blitz for a couple of minutes until you have a smooth, thick mixture. Pass it through a sieve lined with a muslin (cheesecloth) (use a splash more water to swill out the mixer jug and add that too). Leave the milk to drip through (in the fridge), then squeeze out the grounds in the cloth. You should get about 700ml (3 cups) of milk.

Heat the oil in a large saucepan over a low–medium heat. Add the onion, fennel, garlic and a pinch of salt. Stir to coat in the oil, cover and cook, stirring continuously for 15 minutes until all the veg is softened. Add the almond milk, stock and potato and stir everything together. Continue cooking for 10 minutes to ensure the potato is cooked.

Meanwhile, heat a frying pan over a medium heat and dry fry the remaining almonds for about 5 minutes, stirring continuously, until they are golden and smelling toasty. Remove them from the hot pan straight away.

Add half the vanilla to the soup, then blend until smooth. Taste and add a little more vanilla, if you like – you just want an aromatic hint. Season to taste and serve sprinkled with the toasted almonds and a few chopped reserved fennel fronds.

Tiny Little Scallops with
Beetroot & Dill Soup

I'm a real fan of adding flavour afterwards (but not as an afterthought) to what are, fundamentally, classic soups. The scallops are to this what the flaming orange zest is to a Cosmopolitan. Sure, you can enjoy it without, but there's a reason earthy beetroot and sweet scallops are so commonly paired, and these little Patagonian ones are just so conveniently crouton-sized…

SERVES 4

TAKES 1 hr

2 tbsp olive oil, plus a drizzle for the scallops
1 large sweet white onion, diced
2 sticks celery, sliced
500g (1lb 2oz) peeled and diced beetroot (beets)
600ml (2½ cups) vegetable stock
1 x 400ml (14fl oz) can coconut milk
a big bunch of dill, stalks discarded and fronds roughly chopped, plus a few sprigs to serve
sea salt and freshly ground black pepper
1 pack Patagonian scallops, to serve
4 teaspoons Greek yogurt, to serve

Heat the oil in a large saucepan over a low heat, add the onion and celery and cook for about 10 minutes until both are tender. Add the beetroot and cook for 5 minutes more.

Add the vegetable stock and pop a lid on the pan. Raise the heat to medium and cook for about 30 minutes, with the lid on, until the beetroot is tender.

Pour in the coconut milk, then transfer the soup to a blender and add the dill and a good pinch of salt and pepper. Blend until smooth, then taste and add more seasoning if you feel it needs it – it will take quite a lot.

Heat a drizzle of oil in a non-stick frying pan set over a high heat. Once very hot, add the scallops and flash fry for about 3 minutes maximum, turning halfway through, until they are golden and caramelized on the outside.

Pour the soup into warmed bowls and top each with a quarter of the scallops, a teaspoon of yogurt and a few dill sprigs to serve.

Sunshine Basil with
Lemon & Egg Soup

This is a take on the Greek soup avgolemono, only with the basil ante well and truly upped. It may seem odd to add egg to a soup, but you can see a sort of sorcery at play as you stir in the eggs and watch the soup transform from watery broth to thickened, enriched elixir. Make sure you use the very best chicken stock for this – it is the base for the flavour.

 SERVES 4

 TAKES 35 mins

1 tbsp olive oil
20g (1½ tbsp) butter
3 echalion shallots, finely sliced
1 small garlic clove, finely chopped
75g (½ cup) white long-grain rice
1 litre (4 cups) good-quality chicken
   stock (homemade if at all possible
   – see page 11)
2 large eggs
3 tbsp lemon juice
zest of ¼ lemon
a small handful of Greek basil
   leaves, or finely shredded
   normal basil leaves

Heat the oil and butter in a large saucepan set over a low heat and let the butter melt. Add the shallots and the garlic and sauté very gently for about 10 minutes – don't let them colour. Add the rice and stir to coat in the oil, then add the stock and simmer for about 10 minutes, or until the rice is almost tender. Turn the heat off (so you don't forget about it and let it start boiling) while you do the next bit.

Whisk the eggs in a bowl until light, then add the lemon juice and whisk in. Scoop up a ladleful of the hot soup from the pan and trickle it slowly into the egg mixture, whisking as you go. Tempering the eggs like this will stop them curdling when they are added to the pan. Once you've added about 3 ladlefuls in the same way, tip the egg mixture slowly into the soup pan, stirring all the time as you go. Turn the heat back on so it is very low and cook incredibly gently until the eggs begin to thicken the soup a little – do not let it boil or the eggs will scramble. Add the lemon zest and season with salt and pepper.

Just before serving, stir in most of the basil leaves. Ladle the soup into 4 warmed bowls and top each one with a sprinkle of the remaining basil and a good grinding of black pepper.

127

Poached Eggs & Pine Nuts with
Wild Garlic Soup

If you're not entirely sure what wild garlic looks like when it's not picked and packaged in plastic, it's worth doing a quick internet search. It grows quite prolifically in roadside hedges (wash it well) in many parts of the UK, so rather than walking obliviously past it, you could be sitting on a bit of a flavour goldmine. The shock of a vivid orange-yolked egg perched on top of the vibrant green was too fun to resist, but it does make this rather rich, so portions are kept advisedly modest.

 SERVES 4

 TAKES 45 mins

1 tbsp olive oil
1 small onion, finely sliced
700ml (3 cups) vegetable stock
40g (¼ cup) arborio rice
30g (¼ cup) pine nuts
1 tbsp white wine vinegar
250g (about a 10oz packet) frozen
   spinach
150g (5½oz) wild garlic
4 very fresh golden-yolked eggs
sea salt and freshly ground black
   pepper

Heat the oil in a large saucepan set over a low heat. Sauté the onion for 8–10 minutes, until really softening. Add the stock and the rice and cook for 15 minutes, or until the rice still has a little bite.

Meanwhile, dry fry the pine nuts in a small frying pan over a medium heat, stirring continuously, for about 4–5 minutes until they are turning golden and smelling toasty. Tip onto a plate immediately.

Fill a pan about 5cm (2in) deep with water, add the vinegar and bring to a gentle simmer.

Add the frozen spinach to the stock and rice. Cook for about 3 minutes, until the liquid is back up to simmering point. Turn off the heat, add the wild garlic and let it wilt in the heat of the liquid. Transfer to a liquidizer, or blend with a stick blender until smooth. Season with salt and pepper.

method continues overleaf...

Wild Garlic

continued...

Cook the eggs 2 at a time to avoid a big mess. Take the first 2 and crack them into separate small bowls. Gently lower the bowls, one at a time, into the water and tip out the eggs. Allow to cook for 3 minutes, until the whites are set but the yolks remain runny. Using a slotted spoon, remove to a plate lined with kitchen paper. Repeat with the remaining eggs.

Ladle the soup into 4 warmed bowls and top with a poached egg. Sprinkle over the toasted pine nuts to serve.

Pseudo-Swedish
Creamy Fish Soppa

Stockholmers know their seafood. They also know their soup – again, hardly a shock that soup should form part of the survival strategy for enduring austere Scandi noir winters. This is my Frankensoup, pieced together from the memory of the fish soups I tried when I was out there. It may not be exact, but it's pretty tasty anyway, and if you can't find fresh herring (don't try it with marinated herring – it makes the soup unpleasantly vinegary), feel free to use mackerel instead.

 SERVES 4

 TAKES 40 mins

30g (2 tbsp) butter
1 tbsp olive oil
1 onion, diced
1 leek, finely sliced
½ tsp fennel seeds
2 garlic cloves, finely chopped
a good pinch of saffron
150ml (⅔ cup) white wine
1 litre (4 cups) good fish stock
2 tbsp tomato purée (paste)
1 floury potato, peeled and diced into
    1.5cm (⅝in) cubes

Heat a large saucepan over a low heat and add the butter and oil. Once the butter has melted, add the onion, leek, fennel seeds and garlic and sauté gently for 10 minutes until everything is softened.

Meanwhile, put the saffron in a small bowl with a splash of warm water and set aside to soak.

Add the white wine to the saucepan and turn the heat to medium–high. Cook for a few minutes until almost all the liquid has evaporated. Pour in the fish stock and stir in the tomato purée and potato cubes. Bring the liquid to the boil, then lower the heat to a gentle simmer and leave to bubble away for about 20 minutes, or until the potato is tender.

ingredients and method continue overleaf...

Creamy Fish Soppa

continued...

100ml (scant ½ cup) soured cream
200g (7oz) boneless salmon,
  cut into chunks
200g (7oz) boneless herring fillets,
  cut into chunks
450g (1lb) mussels in their shells
a large bunch of dill, chopped
salt and freshly ground black pepper
aïoli, to serve
well-buttered rye bread, to serve

Once the potato is cooked, and with the heat still quite low, add the soured cream, stirring in well until it is fully incorporated. Add the saffron and its soaking water, along with the salmon, herring and mussels, pop the lid back on the pan and cook for about 4 minutes, until all the fish is just cooked through and the mussels have opened. Stir in the dill and season to taste with salt and pepper.

Ladle the soup into 4 bowls (discarding any mussels that haven't opened) and top with a dollop of aïoli. Serve with plenty of buttered rye bread.

Plantain Croutons with Nigerian-inspired
Spicy Peanut Soup

I offer my apologies to anybody reading this who is of Nigerian ancestry as this is almost certainly a mangling of a fine culinary canon. But I stand by it (well, perhaps not my first attempt…). It's got quite a kick, but the peanuts shine through and – as sugar has a magical way of balancing heat – the starchy sweetness of the plantain croutons dampens the fire. Perhaps we can compromise on 'Nigerian inspired'?

SERVES 4

TAKES 50 mins

2 tbsp groundnut oil, plus a drizzle
   for the croutons
1 large onion, diced
3 garlic cloves, finely chopped
2 Scotch bonnet chillies (or more or
   less, depending on how hot you
   want it), sliced
¼ tsp ground cumin
1 litre (4 cups) vegetable stock
450g (1lb) sweet potato,
   peeled and diced
1 large plantain, peeled and diced
4 tbsp 100% natural sugar-free peanut
   butter (I use Meridian)
sea salt and cayenne pepper
dried hibiscus, to sprinkle (optional)

Preheat the oven to 200°C fan/400°F/Gas 6.

Heat the oil in a large saucepan and cook the onion with a good pinch of salt for about 8 minutes, or until softened and translucent. Add the garlic and chillies and cook for a couple more minutes, then add the cumin and fry for another couple of minutes until it's all smelling aromatic. Add the stock and sweet potato to the soup, put a lid on the pan, and let it bubble away for about 15 minutes, or until the sweet potato is tender.

Meanwhile, put the chopped plantain onto a baking sheet, drizzle with a little oil and sprinkle generously with salt. Pop it in the oven and roast for 15–20 minutes, until golden and crisp, stirring halfway through.

Once the sweet potato is cooked, transfer the soup to a blender and liquidize until smooth. Add the peanut butter and season with salt and cayenne pepper, then blitz briefly again. Taste the soup and adjust the seasoning if necessary.

Pour the soup from the blender jug directly into bowls and top with the plantain croutons. Sprinkle with dried hibiscus, if using, to serve.

135

Dukkah with Winter Savory &
Jerusalem Artichoke

If you can't find winter savory, jerusalem artichokes love sage, too, but as savory is said to mitigate some of the more anti-social side effects of artichokes, it's worth hunting it down. Try the local garden centre and plant up what's left of it. Dukkah, a gutsy Middle Eastern spice and nut mix, makes a great sprinkle for the top of the bowl.

SERVES 4

TAKES 30 mins

1 tbsp olive oil

30g (1oz) butter

1 onion, diced

1 large garlic clove, finely chopped

750g (1lb 10oz) jerusalem artichokes,
   peeled and diced

1 medium potato, peeled and diced

1 litre (4 cups) vegetable stock

2 fresh bay leaves

a handful of winter savory sprigs,
   leaves picked and chopped
   (about 2 tbsp)

sea salt and freshly ground
   black pepper

dukkah, to serve

Heat the oil and butter in a large saucepan set over a low heat. Add the onion and garlic. Sauté for a good 8 minutes or so until soft. Add the artichokes and potato and stir to coat in the oil, then add the stock, bay leaves and savory. Pop a lid on the pan and leave to simmer for about 20 minutes, or until the artichokes are tender.

Once the vegetables are cooked, fish out the bay leaves and discard them. Transfer the soup to a blender (or use a stick blender) and blend until very smooth, adding a splash of water if you think it's a bit thick. Quickly pulse in some salt and pepper, then taste and adjust the seasoning if need be.

Pour the soup straight into 4 warmed bowls and top with a sprinkling of dukkah to serve.

Pear Crisps with
Parsnip & Pear Soup

This warmly spiced and deeply comforting soup is at risk of becoming oversweet. You'd expect the sweetness to come from the fruit, but deceptively it's the parsnip that needs to be reined in. Get firm pears and they will add a touch of sharpness and lightness, and prevent this from becoming stodgy. The crisps are a bit of fun; if you don't have a mandoline, don't sweat it – just serve standard croutons.

 SERVES 4

 TAKES 1 hr

4 pears (slightly under-ripe)
1 tbsp olive oil, plus a little for greasing
1 onion, diced
1 garlic clove, finely chopped
500g (1lb 2oz) parsnips, peeled and diced
black seeds from 6–8 cardamom pods, ground in a pestle and mortar
1 litre (4 cups) homemade vegetable stock (see page 13)
a good squeeze of lemon juice
sea salt and freshly ground black pepper

Start by getting the pear crisps baking. Preheat the oven to 100°C fan/200°F/Gas ½ and lightly grease a large baking sheet.

Slice two of the pears (leaving the skin on) thinly on a mandoline – you're aiming for 2mm (⅛in) max thickness. Lay the slices out on the prepared baking sheet and bake for 30 minutes. Turn them over and bake for another 30 minutes until dried (they will crisp up a little more as they cool down).

Meanwhile, heat the oil in a large saucepan set over a low heat and sauté the onion and garlic gently for 10 minutes, until the onion is softened and translucent. Add the parsnips and cardamom and stir together, then add the stock and cook for about 15 minutes until the parsnips are softened.

Meanwhile, peel, core and dice the remaining pears.

Once the soup has had 15 minutes, add the diced pears and cook for 5 minutes more until the pears are softened. Transfer to a liquidizer and blitz until smooth, then taste and season with salt and black pepper and a good squeeze of lemon juice.

Serve the soup in warmed bowls, topped with the pear crisps and another good grind of black pepper.

Hot-smoked Trout
Watercress & Mint Soup

This recipe is based on a soup, akin to this, made by my Mum using the bounty from the local watercress farm when I was a kid. Combined with freshwater trout and garden mint, there's something undeniably English about this, excusing the fact that lemon trees weren't such a common sight along the banks of the River Chess.

 SERVES 4

 TAKES 30 mins

2 tbsp olive oil
1 onion, diced
1 garlic clove, finely chopped
900ml (scant 4 cups) vegetable or
   chicken stock
1 small potato, peeled and diced
300g (10½oz) watercress
60g (2oz) mint, leaves picked
salt and freshly ground black pepper
crème fraîche, to serve (optional)
200g (7oz) hot-smoked trout, flaked,
   to serve

For the lemony shards
1 thick slice of sourdough bread,
   torn into pieces
1 tbsp olive oil
a good pinch of sea salt flakes
finely grated zest of 1 small lemon

Preheat the oven to 190°C fan/375°F/Gas 5.

Heat the oil in a large saucepan set over a low heat and sauté the onion, with a pinch of salt, for 5–6 minutes until beginning to soften. Add the garlic and cook gently for a further 5 minutes, until the onion is soft and translucent.

Add the stock and potato to the pan, cover with a lid and bring to the boil. Once boiling, reduce the heat to medium and leave to simmer, still covered, for about 15 minutes until the potato is cooked.

Meanwhile, to make the lemony shards, put the bread in a bowl with the olive oil. Add the sea salt flakes and toss it all together. Spread the shards out on a baking sheet and bake for 10–12 minutes until golden and crispy. Remove from the oven and stir in the lemon zest. Leave to cool on the sheet.

Once the potato is cooked, uncover the pan. Add the watercress and mint, letting them wilt in the hot liquid for a few seconds. Use a stick blender, or transfer the soup to a liquidizer and blend until very smooth. Season well with salt and pepper.

Divide the soup between bowls and top with a dollop of crème fraîche, the flaked trout and a scattering of lemony shards.

Crunchy Roasted Chickpeas with
Lovage & Ajwain Soup

Lovage has a strong celery-like flavour, which sits surprisingly well with the aromatic, herby flavour of ajwain. They both pack a powerful flavour punch, so the simple roasted and salted chickpeas provide a blandly calming influence.

SERVES 4

TAKES 30 mins

For the roasted chickpeas
1 x 400g (14oz) can chickpeas
   (garbanzo beans), drained
   and rinsed
a drizzle of olive oil
sea salt flakes

For the soup
2 tbsp olive oil
1 onion, diced
2 garlic cloves, finely chopped
1½ tsp ajwain seeds
800ml (3¼ cups) hot vegetable stock
50g (2oz) arborio rice
250g (9oz) garden peas
50g (2oz) lovage leaves
½ tsp lemon zest, plus a squeeze
   of juice
sea salt and freshly ground
   black pepper

To roast the chickpeas, preheat the oven to 190°C fan/375°F/Gas 5.

Put the chickpeas on a baking sheet and drizzle with olive oil. Pop the sheet in the hot oven and roast for about 20 minutes, shaking the sheet a couple of times during cooking, until they are crisp and golden.

Meanwhile, heat the oil for the soup in a large saucepan over a low heat and add the onion, garlic and ajwain seeds. Cook gently for 10 minutes, until the onion is softened and translucent.

Add the stock and rice to the pan and cook for 15 minutes, or until the rice is almost cooked. Add the peas and lovage and bring the liquid to the boil, then cook for 2 minutes, until the lovage is wilted and the peas are tender. Transfer the liquid to a blender, add the lemon zest and blitz until smooth. If the soup's too thick, add a splash of hot water to loosen a little. Taste and season with salt and pepper and a squeeze of lemon juice.

method continues overleaf...

Lovage & Ajwain Soup

continued...

Once the chickpeas are cooked, remove them from the oven and sprinkle with sea salt flakes.

Pour the soup into warmed bowls and sprinkle each bowl with a few chickpeas, serving any extra on the side.

Goat's Cheese & Maple
Spiced Pumpkin Soup

This is thick, sweet, fragrant and totally nourishing. The tangy goat's cheese and a hit of parsley help to add sharpness and freshness and lift it, but on the darkest days, you'd be forgiven for replacing such trimmings with a chunk of warm, crusty bread.

 SERVES 4

 TAKES 1 hr

For the maple seed brittle
a little oil, for greasing
40g (¼ cup) pumpkin seeds
2 tsp maple syrup
a pinch of cayenne pepper
a pinch of sea salt flakes

To make the brittle, preheat the oven to 160°C fan/325°F/Gas 2–3 and grease a non-stick baking sheet with a little oil. Put the pumpkin seeds in a bowl with the maple syrup and add a pinch of cayenne pepper. Mix together, then pour on to the prepared baking sheet. Bake for 10 minutes.

Meanwhile, put the pumpkin on a large baking sheet and drizzle over 2 tablespoons of olive oil. Sprinkle with the spices and a good pinch of salt and pepper. Stir so the pumpkin is well coated.

Once the brittle is ready, remove from the oven. Immediately tip on to a piece of non-stick baking parchment. Sprinkle with sea salt and leave to cool and set. Turn the oven up to 180°C fan/350°F/Gas 4 and roast the pumpkin for 35–40 minutes, or until tender, stirring halfway through cooking.

ingredients and method continue overleaf...

Spiced Pumpkin Soup
continued...

For the soup

700g (1½lb) peeled and diced
   pumpkin or butternut squash
3 tbsp olive oil
1 tsp ground cumin
1 tsp ground cinnamon
1 tsp sweet smoked paprika
1 onion, diced
2 garlic cloves, finely chopped
800–900ml (3–4 cups) veg stock
a squeeze of lemon juice
sea salt and freshly ground
   black pepper
80g (3oz) soft goat's cheese, to serve
chopped flat-leaf parsley, to serve

Towards the end of the pumpkin cooking time, heat the last tablespoon of oil in a large saucepan over a low heat. Add the onion and garlic and sauté gently for 8 minutes, or until well softened. Add 800ml (3¼ cups) of the stock and bring to the boil. Add the cooked pumpkin and leave to simmer for 5 minutes or so. Transfer everything to a liquidizer and blitz until smooth. Add a little more stock and blend again if you feel the soup is a bit thick. Return to the cleaned pan and season with a good squeeze of lemon juice and salt and pepper to taste, and reheat if necessary before serving.

Ladle the soup into bowls and crumble over a little goat's cheese, followed by a little of the maple brittle. Finish with a good grind of black pepper and a sprinkle of parsley to serve.

Cumin with
Simple Creamed Corn

Cornbread fresh from the oven; blackened cobs straight off the barbecue; popcorn on a family film night… I was trying to work out why the most absurdly simple soup in the book is one of the most satisfying and the answer, of course, is its primary ingredient – a taste that's so bound up in childhood memory, its sweetness making it one of the few vegetables kids will eat (almost) without question. There are no added frills that I can think of that will actually improve this soup.

 SERVES 4

 TAKES 30 mins

2 tbsp olive oil
1 onion, roughly diced
1 large garlic clove, finely diced
2 tsp ground cumin
1 litre (4 cups) vegetable stock
500g (1lb 2oz) frozen 'supersweet'
   sweetcorn
sea salt and freshly ground
   black pepper

Heat the oil in a large saucepan over a low heat and add the onion. Sauté for about 5 minutes until beginning to soften. Add the garlic and cumin and cook for another 5 minutes or so until the onion is fully tender.

Add the stock and turn the heat up to high to bring the stock up to the boil. Once boiling, add the sweetcorn and reduce the heat slightly so it is simmering. Leave to bubble away for about 15 minutes, or until the sweetcorn is very tender.

Remove the pan from the heat and blend with a stick blender, leaving a bit of texture, like creamed corn, rather than a completely smooth liquid. You could do this in a blender or food processor too, but use a restrained pulsing rather than a full-on blitz.

Taste and season well with salt and pepper, then ladle into warm bowls and serve exactly as it is.

Coconut & Lemongrass
Malay Squash Chowder

Perhaps 'chowder' is a stretch here, but there aren't many other nouns that immediately conjure that sense of warmth and richness that a singular bowl of this soup can bring. I have left out the shrimp paste (used heavily in traditional Malaysian cooking) to keep it vegan, but you can add it in, if you like. In lieu of it, tamarind and miso pastes help to deepen the flavour.

 SERVES 4–6

 TAKES 50 mins

500ml (2 cups) vegetable stock
1 x 400g (14oz) can coconut milk
4 tbsp thick coconut cream
2 tsp tamarind paste
600g (1lb 5oz) butternut
    squash chunks
1 tbsp cornflour (cornstarch)
½ tbsp coconut palm sugar
1 tbsp white miso paste
sea salt
coriander (cilantro) leaves, to serve

For the spice paste
3cm (1¼in) piece of fresh galangal
2cm (¾in) piece of fresh turmeric
2cm (¾in) piece of fresh ginger
2 tbsp vegetable oil
2 lemongrass stalks
2 garlic cloves
3 echalion shallots, peeled
1–2 dried chillies

Start by making the spice paste. Peel and roughly chop the galangal, turmeric and ginger, then roughly chop the remaining ingredients so they are easier to blend. Blend everything together in a mini chopper or the small bowl of a food processor until you have a smooth paste.

Tip the paste into a large saucepan and cook over a low heat for about 3 minutes, until it starts to smell lovely and aromatic. Add the stock, coconut milk and cream, tamarind paste and butternut cubes and increase the heat to medium. Pop a lid on the pan and bring the liquid to the boil, then lower the heat so that the mixture is simmering and leave it to bubble away for a good 30–35 minutes until the butternut is really soft and tender.

Mix the cornflour with a small splash of water and stir until dissolved, then add this to the soup along with the sugar and miso paste. Stir in and continue to cook gently for a couple more minutes until the soup has thickened slightly, then season to taste with salt.

Ladle the soup into warmed bowls and serve topped with fresh coriander leaves.

Mushroom & Chestnut Soup with
Stilton Rarebit

The chestnut very much takes a supporting role in this soup, but its presence is undeniable, pepping things up with an underlying creamy, nutty richness while the earthy flavour of mushroom and piney scent of rosemary are allowed to sing.

SERVES 4

TAKES 25 mins

20g (1½ tbsp) butter
1 tbsp olive oil
1 large onion, diced
2 large garlic cloves, finely chopped
2 tsp finely chopped rosemary
5 large flat field mushrooms (about 400g/14oz), chopped
800ml (3¼ cups) vegetable stock
200g (7oz) cooked chestnut purée
sea salt and freshly ground black pepper

For the rarebits

4 small or 2 large slices wholegrain sourdough
25g (2 tbsp) butter, softened
½ tsp Dijon mustard
80g (3oz) Stilton or other blue cheese (or vegetarian alternative)
a splash of milk

Put the butter and the oil in a large saucepan set over a low heat and let the butter melt. Add the onion, garlic and rosemary and sauté gently for about 8 minutes until the onion is softened. Add the mushrooms, turn up the heat and continue to cook for a further 5 minutes until the mushrooms are beginning to take on some colour.

Add the vegetable stock to the pan and bring to the boil, then lower the heat and simmer for a few minutes until everything is well cooked.

Meanwhile, toast the bread for the rarebits in a toaster or under a grill (broiler). Put the butter in a bowl and beat in the mustard, then crumble in the cheese and mix until well combined. Add a tiny splash of milk to bring it all together into a spreadable mixture, then spread the cheese over the toast. Set aside until you are ready to serve.

Stir the chestnut purée into the soup, and transfer everything to a liquidizer. Blend until smooth, then taste and season well with salt and pepper.

Just before serving, toast the rarebits under a hot grill for about 2 minutes, or until the cheese is melted and bubbling and turning golden on top. Serve them with the soup for dipping.

Thyme with
Confit Tomato Soup

This soup is an attempt to distil that heady scent of tomatoes at the height of the season when they are at their very best; to concentrate and sweeten that amazing flavour. And while it might seem counterproductive to spend two hours cooking the tomatoes to reduce the liquid and concentrate the flavour, only to then reconstitute it into a soup, this is depth of flavour you can't achieve by boiling up tomatoes and stock.

SERVES 4

TAKES 2 hrs 5 mins

1.4kg (3lb 2oz) very ripe, very red vine tomatoes (about 15 large ones), sliced in half
2 small red onions, halved
4 large garlic cloves, unpeeled
several bushy sprigs of soft summer thyme
4 tbsp olive oil
a pinch of dark brown sugar (you may not need this if the tomatoes are very ripe and sweet)
sea salt and freshly ground black pepper

Preheat the oven to 120°C fan/250°F/Gas 1.

Spread the tomato halves over a large roasting pan, cut side up, and dot the onion halves and garlic cloves in the spaces between. Sprinkle over the thyme sprigs, then drizzle the oil over everything. Sprinkle over the sugar, if using, and a good pinch of salt. Pop in the oven and bake for about 2 hours, or until the tomatoes are well cooked, smell sweet and are beginning to collapse.

Extract the garlic cloves from the pan. Squeeze the garlic cloves out of their skins. Tip the tomatoes, thyme, garlic and any juices in the roasting pan into a liquidizer. Pour 300ml (1¼ cups) of hot water into the roasting pan and use a spatula to scrape any juices and baked bits up off the bottom of the pan. Pour all this into the liquidizer, too. Blend until smooth, adding a splash more hot water if needed to get it to a nice smooth but thick consistency. Taste and season well with salt and pepper.

If necessary, tip the soup into a clean pan set over a low heat and heat gently to rewarm, then serve.

Index